GETTING AHEAD COLLECTIVELY

Pergamon Titles of Related Interest

Related Journals*

GEOFORUM

HABITAT INTERNATIONAL

INTERNATIONAL JOURNAL OF INTERCULTURAL RELATIONS

LANGUAGE AND COMMUNICATION

WORLD DEVELOPMENT

*Free specimen copies available on request.

GETTING AHEAD COLLECTIVELY
Grassroots Experiences in Latin America

Albert O. Hirschman

The Institute for Advanced Study

With photographs by Mitchell Denburg

PERGAMON PRESS

New York Oxford Toronto Sydney Paris Frankfurt

Pergamon Press Offices:

U.S.A. Pergamon Press Inc., Maxwell House, Fairview Park,
Elmsford, New York 10523, U.S.A.

U.K. Pergamon Press Ltd., Headington Hill Hall,
Oxford OX3 0BW, England

CANADA Pergamon Press Canada Ltd., Suite 104, 150 Consumers Road,
Willowdale, Ontario M2J 1P9, Canada

AUSTRALIA Pergamon Press (Aust.) Pty. Ltd., P.O. Box 544,
Potts Point, NSW 2011, Australia

FRANCE Pergamon Press SARL, 24 rue des Ecoles,
75240 Paris, Cedex 05, France

FEDERAL REPUBLIC Pergamon Press GmbH, Hammerweg 6,
OF GERMANY D-6242 Kronberg-Taunus, Federal Republic of Germany

Library of Congress Cataloging in Publication Data

Hirschman, Albert O.
    Getting ahead collectively.

    Incudes bibliographical references and index.
    1. Community development, Urban--Latin American-- Case
studies. 2. Rural development--Latin America--Case
studies. I. Title.
HN110.5.Z9C6267   1984   307'.14'098   84-6487
ISBN 0-08-031616-6

This book is being published as a supplement to the journal, World Development, *Vol. 12 (1984)*

Printed in the United States of America

Contents

Preface

In early 1983, being on sabbatical leave from the Institute for Advanced Study, I spent fourteen weeks in six Latin American countries—the Dominican Republic, Colombia, Peru, Chile, Argentina, and Uruguay—visiting "grassroots development" projects that had obtained financial support from the Inter-American Foundation. My wife Sarah accompanied me throughout, except in Chile and Uruguay, and helped a great deal, through participation in the discussions and note-taking (hence the "we" in my narrative). In each country the representatives of the Foundation introduced us to the community people responsible for the projects, but then left us quite free to develop the conversation and to arrange further contacts. I am most grateful to the Foundation and to its representatives for facilitating our expeditions which often involved complicated logistics. It was not part of my intention to "evaluate" the Foundation and its work. I simply used it as a convenient means of access to the "grassroots" and wish to thank it here for letting itself be so used. But I also want to declare that I have come out of the experience with an enormous admiration for the constructive contribution the Inter-American Foundation has been making to social and economic progress in this Hemisphere. At the present time, the Foundation is passing through a time of troubles not of its own making. One must hope that its usefulness can be preserved.

Upon termination of the field trips, I spent one month in Brazil and there I wrote a draft of most of the following essay. This speedy way of registering my impressions had obvious advantages. The many images I had gathered retained much of their original sharpness and the task of writing was facilitated as a result. More specifically, I am convinced that only in this manner could I have come upon some of the comparative features of the various experiences. But there is also a price for my haste: I was unable to consult the expanding literature on cooperatives and on grassroots development in general. Hence the almost complete absence of references and my refusal to stray outside the set of projects I had visited. All of this makes clear, I hope, how my report should be read: as a reasoned travelogue, rather than as a scholarly treatise.

My greatest debt of gratitude is to the community leaders and members I met in Latin America, for their frankness, patience, hospitality and cordiality. I cannot name them for lack of space, and so I shall similarly forego listing those, inside the Inter-American Foundation and outside, who have given me useful comments on the early draft.

One close reader of this draft deserves special mention, however. He is Mitchell Denburg, whose photographs adorn this book. In the fall of 1983 he travelled with my manuscript to most of the sites I had written about. The pictures he took beautifully evoke the general feeling of these sites; many of them, moreover, provide precise illustrations of specific points made in the text.

Most of Chapter 4 was published separately in *Grassroots Development*, Vol. 7, No. 2, 1983, under the title "The Principle of Conservation and Mutation of Social Energy."

Albert O. Hirschman
January 1984

Introduction

...the desire of bettering our condition...comes
with us from the womb and never leaves us till we
go into the grave.

Adam Smith
The Wealth of Nations

The present essay means to be a commentary, with examples
and even illustrations, on this key statement of Adam Smith.
He issued it as a self-evident axiom that accounts for people's
urge to save. The very term "bettering our condition," like the
more contemporary expressions "getting ahead" or "making
it," seems to point to individual effort. But other patterns of
action serving the same objective must also be considered: they
involve *collective* initiatives such as formation of interest groups
or cooperatives, protests against new taxes or higher prices, or
even the joint occupation of some privately or publicly owned
idle lands near a city by a group of people without adequate
housing. These are also actions people take to "better their
condition" and a fair number of such actions with a collective
dimension took place in Adam Smith's own time (for example,
the Wilkes riots), but in the *Wealth of Nations* they are either
ignored or—in the case of combinations of businessmen—cas-
tigated as "conspiracies against the public."

There is in fact a continuum of actions—from the wholly
private to the most outspokenly public, with many intermediate and hybrid varieties in between—that come under Adam
Smith's rubric: they are all conceived and intended by the participants as means to the end of "bettering their condition."
The question might be asked, therefore, under what conditions
any particular item along the continuum will be chosen. The
scope of the present essay is much less ambitious. Based on
an exposure to a large number of private and collective attempts of people to better their condition, it simply aims at
telling the story of these attempts in some order and with attention to common features and comparative patterns.

Not having had much prior contact with the problems of

"grassroots development," I set out on the expedition with an *open* mind. But at this stage of my life and writings, I can hardly pretend to a *blank* mind: it will not come as a surprise if some of the points to be made here are strongly related to earlier concerns of mine, from certain propositions of *The Strategy of Economic Development* (1958) to my recent interest (*Shifting Involvements*, 1982) in the motivations impelling people toward the pursuit of either the private or the public happiness. In eliciting from, say, the leaders of peasant cooperatives the history of their organizations and an account of difficulties and conflicts, I could not help but be specially attentive to elements of the stories that exhibited some kinship with my "linkages" or, more generally, with sequential solutions to alleged vicious circles.[1] My heart still beats faster when I come upon "wrong-way-round" sequences of the kind I had identified in *The Strategy of Economic Development* or, for that matter, upon new observations bearing upon other themes I have cultivated, such as the exit-voice polarity. Nevertheless, eventually and mercifully, new topics arose out of the rich materials being gathered and they commanded my attention in turn.

Here is, in fact, the pattern which I shall follow in telling my story. I start with observations related to some of my earlier favorite notions, such as certain types of developmental sequences (Chapters 1 and 2). Subsequently, with a composite picture of "grassroots development" slowly emerging, I deal with general themes that are less derivative from my earlier work and do justice to our materials in their own terms (Chapters 3 to 5). Chapter 6 discusses the "intermediate" organizations that have grown up all over Latin America to help low-income people better their condition, and in the concluding chapter I speculate on the social and political effects of a dense network of grassroots development efforts.

---

[1] See my paper "A Dissenter's Confession: *The Strategy of Economic Development* Revisited," to be published in Gerald Meier and Dudley Seers, eds., *Pioneers of Development*, (Oxford University Press, 1984).

Chapter One

Inverted Sequences

I continue to collect inverted, "wrong-way-round" or "cart-before-the-horse" development sequences for a simple reason: the finding that such sequences exist "in nature" expands the range of development possibilities. They demonstrate how certain forward moves, widely thought to be indispensably required as first steps in some development sequence, can instead be taken as second or third steps. From prerequisites and keys to any further progress, these moves are thus downgraded to *effects*, induced by other moves that, so it turns out, can start things going. Perhaps these other moves will be within easier reach of certain societies and cultures than the dethroned "prerequisite." Two examples follow.

IS SECURITY OF TITLE A PRECONDITION FOR HOUSING IMPROVEMENTS? CALI (COLOMBIA) VS. QUILMES (ARGENTINA)

In Cali, the dynamic city in the fertile Cauca Valley in Colombia, a large proportion of the population of 1.5 to 2 million lives in precarious homes, built frequently by the occupants on publicly owned land. Our Colombian guide this time was not an IAF representative, but an official of the local Carvajal Foundation which is heavily involved in helping the squatters by making building materials readily available at reasonable prices. At one point he called my attention to the visible difference in

Cali, Colombia: a new *barrio de invasión* (squatter neighborhood), named after the President of Colombia.

the quality of construction between the houses on the two sides of a street we were passing through. ''The reason is, of course,'' he said, ''that the people on the well-built side have title to their land while those on the other do not.''

The explanation seemed satisfactory enough and I did not give more thought to the matter until we were taken on another such tour, this time in Quilmes, a town 30 kilometers to the east of Buenos Aires that has become part of the Greater Buenos Aires urban sprawl. Here a large area of previously idle land was occupied in 1981 by 1,500 families in what was the largest such invasion ever recorded in Argentina (in Peru collective invasions of this type have been common). The land was immediately subdivided by the organizers of the invasion into regular city blocks which in turn were cut up into individual lots. By the time of our visit, a fair number of wood, brick, and cement block houses had been built or were going up (we visited on a weekend and there was a great deal of hammering

GETTING AHEAD COLLECTIVELY

Above: Cali, Colombia: home with title to land.

Below: Cali, Colombia: home without title to land.

INVERTED SEQUENCES

Quilmes (near Buenos Aires), Argentina: building a first-aid center.

and clanging) to replace the shacks built out of *chapas*, that is, corrugated iron or aluminum sheets and sundry packing crate materials which were used originally. To help increase incomes in the settlement, the IAF had agreed to finance the building of several daycare centers that would free the women for outside jobs, mostly in domestic service. We were led around by various "block delegates"—the squatters had formed an association with a well articulated hierarchical structure: each

GETTING AHEAD COLLECTIVELY

Above: Quilmes: squatter houses made out of *chapas.*

Below: Quilmes: squatter houses built with *materiales.*

block elects a delegate and the delegates in turn elect an executive committee. The block delegates explained to us that progress in building more permanent and "decent" structures (wood, brick and cement blocks are referred to as *materiales* in contrast to the *chapas*) is very important, not only for the sake of the health and comfort of those who live in the structures, but for the survival and prosperity of the community as a whole. The more solidly and respectably built the houses are, the *less* likely it is that the authorities will send bulldozers to demolish the whole new settlement, and the *more* likely does it become that titles to the land will eventually be forthcoming. Various political pressures to that end are already being mounted. So one of the jobs of the block delegates is to encourage the individual squatter families to improve or rebuild their houses, to grow flowers in their front yards and so on. In fact, the delegates pointed out to us with much pride that in some respects the new settlement is steadily gaining on the neighboring community where people have long had title to their land. They even suggested that once you have title, there is hardly any incentive anymore to improve your house—just as, so I added, ownership of a book (in contrast to borrowing with a set return date) often militates against reading it!

I certainly do not want to go too far in this direction. Both Cali and Quilmes exist and yield valuable information on possible sequences. But Quilmes is the more unexpected one—absence of title leads to strenuous efforts to build rapidly and well, as a means of avoiding expulsion and of pressing for title—and therefore deserves to be exhibited at greater length.

EDUCATION IN LITERACY—
PREREQUISITE OR INDUCED?
SOME EXPERIENCES IN COLOMBIA

One of the most characteristic features of the current social scene in Latin America is the ubiquitous presence of so-called "intermediate" organizations that have taken it upon themselves to do "social promotion" (*promoción social*) among the poorer sections in the cities or the countryside. Formed typically by young professionals—lawyers, economists, sociologists, social workers, architects, agronomists, priests, or former priests, etc.—these organizations often attempt to combine research and action. But their principal motivation is to ''go to the people'' and help them, just like the Russian Populists of the 1870s, with the difference that our modern Narodniki are equipped with some technical skills; moreover, after some initial successes, they may be able to enlist outside financial support, frequently on the part of international aid agencies that are also intent on reaching down to the people and are often happy to rely on the local knowledge and contacts of these new kinds of ''middlemen'' or ''brokers'' (See Chapter 6).

In Cartagena, Colombia, we met one such group. Its director, Hugo Aceros, a former priest, now married and with 3 children, had been strongly influenced by a course on the teaching of literacy that he had taken in Bogotá in 1970. The course was offered in conjunction with the then active efforts at pushing land reform and was largely based on the meth-

Hugo Aceros, Director of the *Centro de Alfabetización Temática*, Cartagena, Colombia.

odology of the Brazilian philosopher-educator Paulo Freire. Equipped with that new key to the teaching of how to read and write, Hugo was all set to spread literacy among the peasants and agricultural laborers of the Northern Coast areas around Cartagena. He and his wife set up a small organization of professionals and friends which they grandly called *Centro de Alfabetización Temática* (the ''thematic'' harkens back to one of the principal ideas of the Freire method). But soon they found out that the campesinos of Bayunca, the peasant village near Cartagena with which they first established contact, were not particularly interested in literacy for its own sake—and slowly, talking with them, developed other plans. For example, the group became involved in helping with the acquisition of new land, and in planning for its communal use. In due course, Hugo and his group worked closely with a number of campesino communities on problems of production, legal rights to land, cooperative formation, putting pressure on the authorities for needed public works and similar endeavors that were first priority for the farmers. He is now convinced that

Bayunca, near Cartagena: street scene.

GETTING AHEAD COLLECTIVELY

Bayunca: members of the cooperative.

education is hardly ever the first link in a chain of developmental actions—but has not bothered to change the name of his *centro*. To the extent that education is at all in high demand, it is, he found, for one's children and only indirectly for oneself. Once the campesinos of Bayunca had achieved joint ownership of an additional piece of land they did evince a strong interest in a school for their children; and this school, so they specified, should teach both the usual academic curriculum *and* practical knowledge. The farmers fully expected to profit themselves from the latter. A school has now been built in the community (thanks to an IAF grant) with a curriculum that gives equal time to the three Rs and to instruction in agricultural practices.

We have been strongly conditioned to think that education is a prime mover and a precondition to development. The case just cited shows that the sequence can be the other way round, that education (training in literacy, arithmetic, etc.) will often be *induced by* development. This sort of sequence was very much in evidence in another Colombian situation: in Versalles, a small town sitting on the Eastern slopes of the Western Cordillera, between the Pacific Ocean and the Cauca Valley, a

Bayunca: at the new school.

number of campesinos have joined in a consumer and producer cooperative and this coop has several branches in sur-
rounding *veredas*, that is, remote campesino settlements.
Here we were told that the cooperative, once established,
worked as a powerful tool for education: the campesinos who
were elected to work as administrators and sales people in the
coop tended of course to be among the better educated, but
even so, they found, they had to brush up considerably on
their reading, writing and mainly arithmetic through courses
and homework. The same held for the members who, after an
experience with corrupt administration of an earlier coop, were
now intent on exercising some control.

In such cases, the education of the campesinos could legiti-
mately be considered an "output" of the coop alongside its
performance in providing consumer goods at reduced prices.
The value of this output should therefore be given some attention in estimating the real benefits of such coops. Clearly coops
must break even to survive, but if they do so their social benefit
is likely to be superior to the monetary measure, if only on

account of their educational impact. Later we will discuss other non-monetary benefits as well as costs. In the case of Versalles, the education-inducing role of coops was clearly perceived by one of the local leaders—he used it consciously and successfully in setting up various courses *after* a coop had been established.

Chapter Two

Other Notable Sequences

The inverted sequences of the previous chapter are a special category within a more general class of sequences that are unexpected, unintended, or otherwise notable. Even when not strictly "the wrong-way-round," such sequences have much to teach us about development and social change.

INVENTING A NEW LINKAGE: A *MICROEMPRESA* IN SANTIAGO DE LOS CABALLEROS

In line with my plan of moving from the self-centered to the more general, I start with a sequence that I thought surprising as it contradicted, or at least served to qualify, some ingrained notions of mine. In Santiago de los Caballeros, the second largest city of the Dominican Republic, a free zone for industry was established a few years ago and has had some success in attracting foreign investors. After a lecture at the local university I was asked what I thought of such free zones. I answered that, here and there, they had made valuable contributions to employment creation but that, from my point of view, they are a rather inferior type of investment because they are so antiseptically clean of both backward and forward linkages: typically, the free zone produces strictly value added, with inputs being imported and outputs exported, so that the operation leaves no development stimulus in the country except for the (not negligiblc) incomes that are being generated. It seems to be the industrial equivalent of the agricultural or mineral "enclaves" of an earlier period.

Immediately after this exchange our program called for a visit to various very small enterprises (now known as *microempresas* all over Latin America) located in the poorer sections of the city. The first such venture belonged to a young man who had set up in his home a workshop for producing men's and women's leather belts. Apparently his business was flourishing. I asked him how he had hit on this particular idea and product. The answer was as simple as it was hurtful to my professorial pride: before going into business for himself, so he told us, he had been working in a U.S.-owned firm from Miami that was producing belts for export in Santiago's free zone! This potential transfer of acquired skill and entrepreneurship from the free zone to the domestic economy was a kind of linkage that I had left out of account in my reply to the students.

FROM PRIVATE COOPERATION TO THE PUBLIC ARENA

The next two stories illustrate a number of interesting sequences, principally perhaps the development of group solidarity and public action out of modest and quite private beginnings of cooperative action.

From Debt Pooling to Pressure Group: The Tricycle Riders of Santo Domingo

In Santo Domingo, the capital of the Dominican Republic (population 1.5 million), much of the city-wide distribution of fruits and vegetables, of coal, and of a host of other items is taken care of by some 5,000 *tricicleros* (tricycle riders)—the paired wheels are in front of the rider (rather than in the back as with children's tricycles) and a large rectangular iron rack which holds the merchandise is mounted in between. Most of these *tricicleros* are too poor to own their tricycles: rather they have to rent them for a daily fee which amounts to something like 20% of their average daily earnings. In 1980 the *Fundación para el Desarrollo Dominicano* (FDD), a private development agency formed by local businessmen and socially concerned citizens, consulted about this situation with the Cambridge (Massachu-

Santo Domingo, Dominican Republic: a *triciclero* delivering bananas.

setts)-based *Acción Internacional,* a group supplying technical assistance for the development of *microempresas* in Latin America. Jointly they developed a plan for a loan fund which would permit the *tricicleros* to *buy* their vehicles on the installment plan: but as each individual rider represented an unacceptably high risk this loan fund required that groups (*grupos solidarios*) of five to seven *tricicleros* to be formed and be jointly responsible for everyone's payments. The IAF financed the operation with a grant. Today some 200 such *grupos solidarios* exist. Some of the first groups that have been formed are already paid up and their members now own their means of livelihood for the first time.

But this improvement in individual welfare is by no means the end of the story. At the level of social interaction, we were told, the arrangement tended to create close friendships (before the arrangement ''I used to see him around, but I didn't *know* him'' as one *triciclero* put it)—as well as probably some new conflicts. At the level of social organization, the effect was even more remarkable: once a number of *grupos solidarios* was formed, the idea arose to create a tie among the individual

GETTING AHEAD COLLECTIVELY

groups (each of which had an internal structure, with a President, Treasurer, Secretary, etc.) and an Association of Tricycle Riders (or rather of the *grupos solidarios*) came into being. The Association has its own President, Treasurer, etc. and this executive group meets once a week by itself and on another day of the week with the whole membership. The meetings are lively and well attended. The Association soon developed some new activities of its own: it organized a rudimentary health insurance scheme and promoted contributions of members to funeral expenses for members and their immediate family, as an expression of solidarity. Plans are being prepared for

Santo Domingo, Dominican Republic: meeting of the Association of *Tricicleros*.

a tricycle repair shop, with tools and spare parts to be available to members. Increasingly, moreover, the Association began to act as an interest and pressure group, for example by taking a stand against certain measures of the municipal traffic and police departments which often make the harsh life of the *tricicleros* even harder through various taxes, prohibitions, fines, and so on. As we were leaving, a protest against one such measure was being planned. "I can mobilize 500 tricycles to converge on any spot in the city and paralyze everything," said one of the Association's leaders, proud of their new found strength.

In this manner a financial mechanism originally designed to do no more than protect a lending agency against default by individual borrowers is having powerful and largely unanticipated social, economic and human effects, enhancing group solidarity and stimulating collective action.

From Sewing to Advocacy:
A Women's Academy in Comas (Lima)

Comas is an overgrown *pueblo joven* (young town), the "positive" term that was coined in Peru during the Velasco regime, instead of the derogatory *barriada*, for the sprawling, largely self-built urban squatter settlements around Lima and other Peruvian cities. Comas numbers anywhere from 300,000 to 500,000 people and is by now an organized municipality. But conditions of life remain rudimentary and public utilities (with the exception of electric power) are highly deficient. In the center of this huge settlement a Catholic church functions with, next to it, a hall suitable for public meetings.

Here we met a group of women who have organized an "Academy for Women" that holds courses one evening every week during the academic year, which in Peru starts in April and ends in December. The venture started four years ago when some women in Comas got together to look for ways of increasing the family income by learning how to sew and to make patterns. In the process they established contact with a *promoción social* group in Lima called *Centro de Estudios Sociales y Publicaciones*. This center was staffed by educators who had been working in official agencies during the early, reform-rich years of the Velasco Administrations and, when disillusioned or simply laid off later on, decided to stay to-

Comas (near Lima), Peru: sewing class at "Academy for Women."

gether as a private group. First they published an educational
magazine for children, but found that they could not make it
financially. Later they shifted to various educational projects,
primarily in the *pueblos jovenes,* with some financial support
of Dutch and German aid agencies. In Comas they provided
the requested assistance for clothesmaking, but quite soon
other topics of instruction were developed in collaboration with
the Comas women: classes in literacy, in the history of Peru,
in female health and sexuality and so on—until a whole curriculum took shape. After two years of instruction by personnel
supplied by the Centro, some topics of instruction were taken
over by the Comas women who had graduated from the course
and felt they could handle the materials themselves. Today the
administration of the Academy and most of the teaching is
handled by these women. Gradually, the women have developed contacts with other women's groups in Comas and a
Comas-wide women's group which discusses feminist issues
has been started. One of the biggest problems the Academy is
facing is the hostility of some husbands to their wives' not

being at home one evening per week. The Academy has attempted to assuage the husbands by drawing them into its activities—organizing, for example, fiestas and common educational events.

What is more, the community women who now run the Academy have recently participated (and have asked the "students" to participate) in various petitions and demonstrations for improvements in the water supply in their district and throughout Comas. Fittingly, the latest course they have added to the Academy's curriculum is entitled "The Place of Women in Politics."

Here then is another sequence where the traditional concern with "bettering one's condition" in the private sense leads over, almost effortlessly and without any clear sense of a break, into public advocacy and participation in public affairs.

COLLECTIVE VENTURES AND PRIVATE LIVES

Now to the opposite movement. Actually it would be more correct to say "nearly opposite" for I shall not be concerned here with any total privatization that would be in some sense the outcome of collective actions. Rather, I shall give an account of two situations where some important and unexpected effects of cooperative or joint action consisted in the impact of that action on the private lives and relationships of the cooperators.

What Will They Do with Their Free Time? The Dairy Plant in Durazno (Uruguay)

In Uruguay I was taken to an active and dynamic agricultural cooperative (*sociedad de fomento rural*) with headquarters in Durazno, a provincial capital some 150 miles north from Montevideo. The latest and most ambitious IAF-financed project of the cooperative is a dairy plant which, so it is hoped, will encourage milk production—because the plant will offer an assured market for the many small and medium-sized local producers of the area—as well as consumption because the milk will now be pasteurized (and attractively packaged). The plant also produces butter and cheese, the latter mostly for export.

Dairy plant at Durazno, Uruguay: making cheese.

We talked a great deal about the prospective profitability of the plant which turned largely on the hoped for, gradual increase in milk deliveries by local producers and on the prospects for cheese exports.

One effect of the new plant was mentioned only casually, toward the end of our visit: the time gained by the local producers as a result of the new arrangement. Before the plant came into production in 1982, most of the local milk producers in the area distributed their own milk—they made daily trips on horsecart to their individual customers as well as to the stores in town. In the spring and summer two daily trips were often necessary because of the larger amount of production and the danger of spoilage. Now a truck from the new plant would collect the milk at the farmer's doorstep thereby saving him from 1 to 5 hours every single day of the year! What would the dairy farmers do with all that free time? Start sowing new crops? Improve their pastures and increase their herds? Devote themselves more to home and family?

Clearly the dairy plant would have a major impact on the

Above: Durazno: family milking cows in afternoon.

Below: Durazno: delivering milk by horsecart.

GETTING AHEAD COLLECTIVELY

welfare of the small dairy farmers of Durazno province. It was also likely to raise the social *esteem* in which these farmers are held. Now they are associates of a much admired, technologically progressive undertaking, whereas previously their daily milk-peddling treks caused them to be viewed as quite lowly members of rural society.

Durazno: unloading milk from truck at dairy plant.

The Effect of Education on Family Ties: A Rural School in Alto Chelle (Chile)

The Durazno story leads to another where the potential effect of a project on family and human relationships holds an even more prominent place. In Alto Chelle, a rather poor agricultural community with widely scattered small holders, located in Southern Chile not far from the city of Temuco, the IAF has been supporting an unusual community-initiated project in rural education. Here some of the more prosperous farmers had long wanted to do something for the progress of their community. First, they organized short courses in gardening, bee-keeping and the like. This was done with the help of the *Instituto de Educación Rural* (IER), a Christian-inspired institution that has been operating in Chile since 1955 and has one of its regional offices in Temuco. Through the IER the community leaders then came into contact with a Franco-Argentinian educator who had had experience in Argentina with a special educational formula for rural areas that had been invented in France in the thirties and had since become an international movement: after elementary school, in seventh and eighth grade and perhaps beyond, children whose parents are practicing farmers alternate throughout the academic year a period of one or two weeks in school, where they would be taught about agriculture along with traditional subjects, with two weeks at home.[2] When at home they would apply some of the knowledge acquired at school (where there are facilities for cultivating plants, handling animals, etc.) and this special kind of "homework" would be regularly inspected by the teaching staff. The proclaimed objective of the system is a dual one: to avoid the alienation from agricultural work that is frequently the result of prolonged schooling in purely academic matters; and to transfer the knowledge of modern agricultural

[2] In France, there are now 500 rural schools (*Maisons Familiales Rurales*) which have adopted this method. The rhythm originally chosen and still in use in France calls for one week in school alternating with two at home. There exist 240 such schools in other countries, mostly in Italy, Spain, and French-speaking Africa. The work of this educational movement is coordinated by the Union Nationale des Maisons Familiales Rurales d'Education et d'Orientation (59, rue Réaumur, 75002 Paris). A good description of the movement, its history and philosophy is in Daniel Chartier, "Naissance d'une philosophie de l'alternance," *Mésonance*, I (1978), pp. 9–189.

The Alto Chelle School, Temuco, Chile: students in vegetable garden.

practices from the children to the parents as the children apply the knowledge acquired at the school to projects at home.[3]

The Alto Chelle community leaders became enthusiastic

[3] In the book cited in preceding footnote, Chartier states that the work-at-home periods serve, among other things, "to invite the young farmer to carry out certain experiments at home so as to break down (*bousculer*) the routine of the parents" (p. 125). But this objective is not at all stressed in the pamphlets published by the Union Nationale des Maisons Familiales Rurales. Since an important purpose of this literature is to make adepts for the system, it may be surmised that the objective of educating the parents through the children is not prominently displayed to avoid offending those who have a capital role to play in setting up new schools. In Chile, on the contrary, the educational effect of the school on the parents was emphasized by all concerned.

about having this sort of school established; land and buildings for the purpose were donated by the Catholic parish and the local leaders contributed considerable time and energy to planning activities. The school was placed under the control of the IER, but a *corporación de padres* (parents' association) formed at the same time in Alto Chelle was eventually to take over the supervisory role.

At the time of our visit, the school had been functioning for over two years. It had its share of administrative and financial difficulties, the major problem being to obtain financial aid from the Ministry of Education so as to end the IAF subsidy. Once established and properly certified, the school is entitled to state aid in principle, but various delays had occurred.

From the educational point of view, we heard nothing but praise about the school which adopted a pattern of alternating two weeks at school with two at home. The parents we interviewed were genuinely pleased with the help they were getting from the children. They were anxious to send all of their children to the school, in spite of the cost (or the loss of labor) this

Alto Chelle: student at home instructing mother in animal care.

Alto Chelle: students
and teacher treating
cow for broken leg.

implied. They also admitted to having learned something from
the children: bee-keeping, the growing of asparagus and some
other vegetables, and how to inject cows and other farm animals with various vaccines.

At a nearby high school, we then interviewed some students
who were alumni of the Alto Chelle school. They were proud
of having gone to this school (in part because it is so special)
and felt it should go on for more than just two years. One

result of the working weeks at home was, so they said, that they got to know their parents much better. Some of these high school students, perhaps 15 or 16 years old, thought that a new friendship with their parents was one of the major benefits of the educational venture in which they had participated. We felt that it would be this closer relationship that might motivate some to return to the land at the end of their education, not only the specialized agricultural knowledge acquired at the Alto Chelle school.

Finally the school is remarkable for the nature of the community's involvement. Because of their many children, the poorer farmers of the area, many of whom are of Mapuche Indian background, are the principal beneficiaries of the school. But the community leaders who have been so active and devoted in promoting the school are the better-off farmers, many of whom are single or widowed women without children. Originally they had sought to improve their community by activities that would benefit themselves as well as others; as it happened, in the course of their contacts with IER, their interest was caught by this school venture which represents an almost wholly altruistic activity for the leader group. Perhaps it is this feature—and the ensuing wonderment over selfless devotion—that make this project into the great favorite of the successive IAF representatives dealing with Chile!

Chapter Three

The Emergence of Cooperative Action: Outside Aggression

So far I have examined a number of sequences and meanderings of grassroots development-in-action that struck me with particular force, largely on the basis of some earlier interests and positions of mine. But time has come to look at my "materials in their own terms," as I put it earlier. A basic question that arises out of the manifold experiences I have learned about concerns, in fact, a special kind of sequence: that which leads to the emergence of the collective endeavors which I have been primarily surveying here. How do these efforts typically arise?

My answer will be in two parts. In this chapter I shall look at those experiences where collective action is provoked by some common, usually adverse, experience to which a group of people is subjected. These people, without much contact with one another before this outside shock, are now brought forcibly together. It is no great mystery why they should take common action, but it is worthwhile looking at the varieties of such actions in some detail. The more difficult question is: under what conditions will people take common action when no such outside pressure can be detected? A partial answer will be attempted in the next chapter.

AGGRESSION BY NATURE:
FLOODING IN ARGENTINA
AND EROSION IN URUGUAY

People can be subjected to aggression either by the hostile forces of nature or by the often even more hostile forces of State and society. We came across a large number of such aggressions that led to the development of solidarity and, eventually, to joint action.

It is plausible enough for aggressions of nature to bring the

La Merced, near Córdoba, Argentina: the water tower.

La Merced: building an addition.

victims together, but the opposite *sauve-qui-peut* reaction is also common. Sudden catastrophes, like earthquakes, tend to be of the latter type, so it seems to me, whereas more slowly proceeding punishments by nature leave time for discussing remedies and for shaping some collective response. This was the case when the waters of a river near the city of Córdoba (Argentina) were rising and threatened the poorly built houses of some laborers employed in nearby farms and quarries who had been squatting near the river, some 3 miles from the nearest urban settlement. They had to make a decision to relocate and now resolved to stay together, farther away from the river, but still close to their sources of livelihood. They found some idle land farther inland, occupied it and cut down the tall weeds jointly. Then they distributed the land among themselves and built themselves new homes. In the process, they became a community of some 60 families.

Their biggest need in the new location of La Merced was water which they had to fetch from the river or which was delivered quite unreliably and expensively by truck. Eventually, the Córdoba-based organization AVE (*Asociación para la Vivienda Economica*), an architect-led *promoción social* agency, made contact with the group. AVE's principal expertise is in housing construction and improvement, but it had come to realize in the course of its work over the years that housing is not always the principal need in either urban or rural slums (See Chapter 6 for a general account of AVE's work). A house-to-house survey, carried out by the people of La Merced themselves, established that water supply was indeed by far their first priority need. With the help of a grant from the IAF, a tall water tower, its size quite out of proportion with the tiny self-built houses, had been erected and was almost ready to function at the time of my visit. The men were feverishly completing the distribution net by digging the ditches where the pipes would be laid. The community, already constituted as a formal cooperative, was also planning an irrigated area where vegetables would be communally grown as a cash crop. Moreover, now that the water problem would be solved, arrangements were being made to receive an additional 40 members.

Soil erosion in its various forms is another case of aggression by nature (even though it is often nature's reaction to man's earlier aggression against it) that acts rather slowly and thus permits a prolonged collective search for remedies. In the Uruguayan Department of Canelones, near Montevideo, small and medium farmers had long permitted their land to be overgrazed or to be sown to wheat year after year without the nutrients being returned to the soil. As a result of the ensuing soil depletion many farmers in the Northeastern part of the Department faced deteriorating conditions. They tried various ways of countering progressive impoverishment: the current favorite is the growing of alfalfa on the depleted soil. Alfalfa is a valuable crop for the feeding of horses and other animals during the winter months. Being a legume as well as a grass that renews itself from the rhizomes for some 3 years, alfalfa returns nitrate to the soil for a prolonged period so that depletion is counteracted.

The need for cooperative action arose here from some special characteristics of the crop. The alfalfa which is quite bulky needs to be stored in a dry place after the harvest. Thus it became necessary to build large sheds in the alfalfa-growing areas and this task, along with the provision of services, was

Above: Canelones, Uruguay: soil erosion.

Below: Canelones, Uruguay: plowing under alfalfa to enrich the soil.

Canelones, Uruguay: alfalfa in shed.

undertaken by a regional grouping of Rural Promotion Socie-ties (*Sociedades de Fomento Rural*) to which most farmers be-long. These societies joined forces to form the Federation of the Northeast of Canelones which provides coordination for the alfalfa plan and has obtained a grant from the IAF for the financing of the sheds. The Federation is the only grouping of its kind in Uruguay.

AGGRESSION BY SOCIETY

Aggression by nature is less prominent in our collection of stories than aggression by man. The latter takes several forms: aggression by sharp operators, by powerful individuals or groups, and by the State.

It is well known that most of the victims of crime are poor people. But the poor suffer aggression not only as individuals: it takes a *group* of poor people to make an attractive target for unscrupulous practitioners planning fraudulent schemes on a large scale. Occasionally it happens then that the common experience of having been taken advantage of, swindled or otherwise hurt will lead to some collective reaction that takes the perpetrators by surprise. This is also true for aggression by powerful individuals or by the State. The poor are used to their poverty which they bear in silence and isolation, but the fact of being treated with *injustice* can bring out unsuspected capacities for indignation, resistance and common action.[4]

Land Swindles: Argentina and Colombia

In Quilmes, in a different section of the already noted suburb of Buenos Aires, a group of poor people settled and built their own homes in a large open terrain around 1963.[5] They were persuaded to do so by the "owner" who "sold" individual lots for reasonable prices to be paid in reasonable installments. The hitch was of course that he was not the owner, a fact that became public knowledge sometime in 1967–68. With everyone having been taken in equally, a new feeling of indignant solidarity arose that led the people of the community to set up, through elections, a Land Commission (*comisión de tierras*) whose task it is to negotiate with the authorities about the title to the land. These negotiations have been long and tortuous, but some progress has been achieved: the land has by now been bought by the state from the real owners, but title is yet to be transferred to the individual occupants—agreement has to be reached on the extent to which the earlier payments to the fictitious owner will be taken into account. At the same time, the group has started a number of other joint activities, with the cooperation of various activist priests: public utilities, from water supply to sidewalks, have been improved, and a meeting place has been communally built, with the financial assistance of NOVIB, the Dutch aid organization. Most recently the community has organized some cultural and educational

[4] See also Barrington Moore, *Injustice: the Social Bases of Obedience and Revolt* (White Plains, N.Y.: M.E. Sharpe, 1978) and John Gaventa, *Power and Powerlessness: Quiescence and Rebellion in an Appalachian Valley* (Oxford: Clarendon Press, 1980). Charles Tilly speaks of "defensive mobilization" in his *From Mobilization to Revolution* (Reading, MA: 1978), pp. 73 ff.

[5] A full account of the episode is in María del Carmen Feijoó, "Las luchas de un barrio y la memoria colectiva," *Estudios CEDES*, Vol. 4, No. 5 (Buenos Aires: 1981), pp. 5–37.

San Bernardo del
Viento, Caribbean
coast, Colombia:
Members of *Liga de
Agricultores El Castillo*
enact how their fathers
were deprived of their
land by the *turco*.

GETTING AHEAD COLLECTIVELY

activities, with guidance from CEDES, a well-known Argentine research organization in the social sciences.

A similar experience in a rural setting comes once again from the northern region of Colombia, close to the Caribbean. In the twenties, near the small town of San Bernardo del Viento in the Department of Sucre, a group of peasant families had been gradually dispossessed of much of their land by the maneuvers of a non-native landowner, a *turco* (this is not necessarily derogatory term used for immigrants, mostly from Syria and Lebanon, many of whom have come to occupy important positions in commerce and industry in much of Latin America). This man died in the mid-sixties without any apparent heir; his relatives in town removed all the "movables," including the cattle, and the land became idle. At that point the peasants at the edges of the hacienda took over the land that was originally theirs or their parents' and began to work it once again. Altogether some 200 peasant families are involved. Then in 1978, an alleged heir appeared, assisted by an influential lawyer from the nearby town of Lorica.

The lawyer intimated that he was going to go to court to recover the land for his client. In the community everyone was convinced that the "heir" story was a complete hoax, but somehow the lawyer was able to achieve what had probably been the objective of the operation from the beginning: not so much to gain posession of the land, but to convince the authorities of the potential for trouble so that they would pay good money for having the matter choked off. INCORA, the Colombian Agency for Land Reform, duly bought the title so as to avoid "social unrest" and was then set to resell the land to the peasants who were on it already. The latter, however, had in the meantime become quite militant in their determination not to lose their land for a second time. "We shall neither hand over the land nor pay for it" became their slogan. They formed an association (*Liga de Agricultores El Castillo*) and looked for outside help. A group of Benedictine fathers from nearby San Bernardo del Viento soon supplied not only moral support, but counsel and further outside contacts. SENA, the official Colombian agency for vocational education, set up courses in cooperativism. And the Inter-American Foundation provided funds for building a meeting place and for paying the expenses of retaining a lawyer for the group, in its fight to keep the land.

Alberto López Tunco,
President of the *Liga de
Agricultores El Castillo*.

In the course of this struggle to resist outside conspiracy and
aggression, the *Liga* undertook a number of new tasks: some
land was made available for communal grazing, a small dam
was built, a consumer store was being planned and, most important perhaps, the art of discussion and joint decision-making was being slowly acquired.

GETTING AHEAD COLLECTIVELY

Harvesting rice in El Castillo.

The State as Aggressor:
Argentina and Chile

In several cases the villain who arouses the dormant cooperative spirit of a group is not some individual crooked operator, but that old-time aggressor: the State. An example comes from Argentina where the military regime that took over in 1976 had made up its mind to rid the central areas of Buenos Aires of the "unsightly" *villas miserias* (or self-built slum housing) that had infiltrated here and there. The operation was conducted with military precision as warnings were issued one day and bulldozers appeared the next to tear down the often flimsily built shacks. Most of the inhabitants of these *villas* simply relocated themselves as best they could, but some of them resolved to stay together and to start new cooperative housing projects. In this endeavor they were helped by an Argentine Foundation called *Fundación Vivienda y Comunidad* and staffed by architects and social scientists, with a dynamic Catholic Priest, Rev. José M. Meisegeier, S.J., known as Padre Pichi, as the guiding spirit. With the assistance of funds supplied in part by the Inter-American Foundation, the *Fundación*, has been able to relocate some 200 families in three different areas, rather far from the central city. These families built their new houses as a cooperative venture. This collective reaction to the military government's brutal assault on the *villas* was limited to a small fraction of the total number of people whose homes were destroyed.

The Chilean military regime that came to power in 1973 supplies an example of the State acting as aggressor on a much larger scale *and* of calling into life, as an unintended result, a major social movement organized by the victims. In 1979, the Pinochet Government issued a law on the division of the Mapuche lands (Decree-Law 2568 of March 22, 1979). The Mapuche are a group of about 500,000 Indians living in the south of Chile, mostly dedicated to agricultural pursuits on poor lands. Some of them have become more or less absorbed into the ways of Chilean society and have individual title to a piece of land. But large groups of Mapuches continue to hold land in common and to work parts of it communally. The 1979 law was designed to do away with all this pre-capitalist "irrationality." Following the official, if imported, doctrine about the universally superior virtue of private over any other form of property, and probably with an eye toward profitable tourist "development" of some of the Mapuche-held lands once they would become available for sale, the government made it extremely easy and attractive for communally-held lands to be subdivided.

According to the new law, an agricultural development agency of the Chilean government (INDAP—*Instituto de Desarrollo Agro-Pecuario*) was to liquidate any community and to issue titles to individual parcels wherever just one occupant of land within the community—Mapuche or otherwise—re-

Padre ''Pichi'' of the Housing and Community Foundation *(Fundación Vivienda y Communidad)*, Buenos Aires, Argentina.

A Mapuche couple, near Temuco, Chile.

quested such subdivision. Further, the Government biased the decision powerfully in the direction of subdivision, by holding out the promise of credit, which was not available to the communities. Moreover, there was the temptation of ready cash, in amounts never before seen by the Mapuche, in case they wanted to sell their individual parcels after subdivision. Given these overwhelming pressures, a number of communities did in fact subdivide.

What is notable is that many others resisted what they called the "surrender" (*entrega*) of their land and resolved to fight it by creating, shortly after the law was issued, an association of Mapuches called AD-MAPU[6]. According to some long-time students of the Mapuche, AD-MAPU has achieved a previously unequalled influence in the Mapuche communities. It has established ties with a Latin-America-wide organization in defense of Indian Rights (CISA—*Consejo Indio-Sudamericano*) and is conducting programs of technical assistance in agricul-

[6] The full name is *Asociación Gremial de Pequeños Agricultores y Artesanos*—AD-MAPU (Association of Small Farmers and Artisans—AD-MAPU).

Mapuche woman cultivating communal land.

ture, training in handicrafts, and promotion of Mapuche culture. For these programs AD-MAPU has received some funding from British and Dutch aid agencies, as well as from the Inter-American Foundation.

We visited one group of Mapuche participating in these programs, who are receiving some educational and other assistance from a group of Chilean anthropologists, and who have formed a study center in Temuco, the southern provincial capital that is close to Mapuche territory. Our conversation with the remarkably articulate group of Mapuche men and women left us with the feeling that resistance to the destruction of communal land tenure was strong and that the policies of the military government had served, at least in this community, to create a new feeling of solidarity and desire for collective advance.

Chapter Four

The Emergence of Cooperative Action: Prior Mobilization

As I said at the outset of the last chapter it is no great mystery why people who are jointly and newly oppressed either by the forces of nature or by their "fellow men" should take some joint action and develop a spirit of solidarity which then leads to further cooperative efforts. After all, they are only conforming, if in collective form, to the French adage:

> *Cet animal est très méchant*
> *Quand on l'attaque il se défend.*
> (This animal is very mean
> When it's attacked it will hit back.)

We now turn to a more difficult inquiry: understanding collective efforts at grassroots development when no immediately antecedent aggression is present.

THE PRINCIPLE OF CONSERVATION AND MUTATION OF SOCIAL ENERGY

I shall not attempt here to account systematically for these more complex situations.[7] However, a large number of them shared one striking characteristic: when we looked into the life histories of the people principally involved, we found that most of them had previously participated in other, generally

[7] See references in note 4.

more "radical" experiences of collective action, that had generally not achieved their objective, often because of official repression. It is as though the protagonists' earlier aspiration for social change, their bent for collective action, had not really left them even though the movements in which they had participated may have aborted or petered out. Later on, this "social energy" becomes active again but is likely to take some very different form. It may therefore be quite difficult to notice that we have here a special kind of sequence, a *renewal* of energy rather than a wholly new outbreak. I shall refer to this phenomenon as the Principle of Conservation and Mutation of Social Energy.

Far be it from me to claim anything like universal validity for this principle. The "normal" reaction to failed collective action is unlikely to be a repetition of such action. Rather it is discouragement, despair, or, at best, a turn toward the active pursuit of *private* happiness.[8] Yet the Latin American experiences that will be recorded shortly remind me—half in contrast, half in parallel—of related themes. First of all, of an old song celebrating the failed German peasant war of the sixteenth century whose last verse reads:

Geschlagen ziehen wir nach haus
Unsere Enkel fechten's besser aus.

(Vanquished we are returning home

Our grandchildren will take up our fight with better luck.)
The difference between our principle and this text is, first of all, that the present Latin American generation is not waiting for their grandchildren: they seem perfectly able to resume a "fight" (that is, to join in some collective movement) several times in the same lifetime. In part this may be due to what has been called the acceleration of history. Perhaps it has more to do with the second and more important difference between the Latin American and the German situation: the Latin Americans are not taking up the same "fight" again; the next time around, they involve themselves in a very different cause.

I am also reminded of a much more contemporary experience: according to a recent study of postwar entrepreneurship in France, a number of the more successful and innovative

[8] See, for an attempt at a description of this turn, my book *Shifting Involvements: Private Interest and Public Action,* (Princeton: Princeton University Press, 1982), Chapter 8.

postwar business ventures, particularly in the field of services, were started by people who had previously been strongly involved with Left-wing or revolutionary politics.[9] Examples are the well-known Club Méditerranée; the FNAC, a multiple-branch discount house with a particularly complete stock of books and records; and Le Point-Mulhouse, a successful travel agency organizing charter flights to faraway places. Interestingly, the character of these enterprises retains a link to the erstwhile political ideals of their founders—for example, the organization of life in the vacation colonies of the Club Méditeranée clearly draws on socialist communal utopias, such as Fourier's *phalanstère*.

At this point, a further related experience comes to mind. As is well known, it was a group of followers of another early 19th century French socialist thinker, the Count of Saint-Simon, that undertook, in mid-century, industrial, railroad, and banking projects on a grand, often transnational scale, more than two decades after their conversion to the Count's doctrines. Here also, unsuccessful advocacy of a set of ideas about needed social change was to be followed by highly successful entrepreneurial activity. There has been much discussion, starting with Marx and Engels, whether the capitalistic activities of the Péreire brothers and of other Saint Simonians under Napoleon III constituted an application or a betrayal of the master's doctines; the correct answer is probably a bit of each. What is undeniable is that the early propagandistic efforts and the later entrepreneurial ventures are activities of a very different kind, yet with a strong internal link.

SOME COLOMBIAN EXAMPLES

In the grassroots experiences we observed in Latin America, the principle of conservation and mutation of social energy assumed a variety of distinctive shapes. The most massive evidence comes from Colombia and perhaps the best illustrative

[9] Jacques Guyaz, ''Innovations dans le secteur des services: du militant à l'entrepreneur,'' in Jean-Daniel Reynaud and Yves Gafmeyer, eds., *Français, qui êtes-vous?* (Paris: La documentaton française, 1980), pp. 191–201. See also, for a more extended version, J. Guyaz, *Les innovateurs et leurs innovations,* unpubl. doctoral thesis (Fondation nationale des sciences politiques, 1981).

Village of Cristo Rey, Caribbean coast, Colombia.

story is that of the fishermen's cooperative at the small settlement of Cristo Rey on the country's Caribbean Coast. From Montería, the hot interior capital of the Department of Córdoba, we drove along rich and sparsely cultivated haciendas to the coast. There we met with a group of fishermen in a round, well ventilated, open shed with a thatched roof. Being of European background, we took for granted that we were dealing with a people that had been fishermen for generations. But we soon learned that, like the rest of the villagers, the coop members had grown up as agriculturalists, each tending a small plot of his own and working on nearby haciendas as day-laborers.

How did they become fishermen? It turned out to be a remarkable story. In 1975, a group of peasants from the village invaded a piece of land that had been idle for a long time, with the idea of working it collectively. They undertook this action toward the end of a period of fairly widespread peasant unrest and land invasions, particularly in the flatlands near Colombia's Atlantic coast. This period of peasant activism followed the more vigorous application of the land reform law of 1961 in the late 1960s under President Carlos Lleras Restrepo and the simultaneous establishment of a peasant union (ANUC = *Asociación Nacional de Usuarios Campesinos*) that was conceived by Lleras as a way for peasants to participate more actively in the reform. Soon enough this union became independent from government tutelage and developed considerable momentum and following. By 1975, however, the political situation had changed substantially: the agrarian reform had been brought to a halt; and ANUC had lost strength as a result of internal divisions. Not surprisingly, therefore, police ejected the Cristo Rey peasants from the land they had sought to cultivate.

But this is not the end. For the next few years the peasants kept in touch, often wondering what next might be done jointly. At one point, looking out on to the Caribbean and noticing some fishing boats in the distance, they said to each other: ''As long as we cannot take the land, why not take the

Fishing boats of Cristo Rey cooperative.

GETTING AHEAD COLLECTIVELY

Cristo Rey cooperative directors meet with SENA staff member (man on right).

sea?'' So the 22 peasants who were closest to each other as a result of joint action (and no doubt other ties) decided to build two boats and set out to sea. Then they mobilized various kinds of assistance, from courses in cooperativism given at Montería by *Acción Unida* (an evangelical social action group), to credit from the *Caja Agraria* (the agricultural credit bank), and accounting courses from SENA (the wealthy and always helpful national vocational training agency). A major step forward was the acquisition of outboard motors—financed by an IAF grant—that permitted the crews to venture much further out to sea and significantly increase production.

The coop has been a financial success. After some time it was able to expand its activities by setting up a consumer store which also houses freezers for the catch. The coop recently bought a sizable piece of land close to the sea where a meeting hall, offices, consumer store, and other activities are to be concentrated. (A fish restaurant and small hotel are in the planning stage!) Another project, currently under consideration by the

The Cristo Rey cooperative consumer store.

IAF, is to expand the "fleet" from the present two to eight boats. Most movingly, the coop members, true to their original vocation as agriculturalists, now think of *renting* some land from a nearby landowner and of cultivating it collectively. As a cooperative, with a "legal personality" (*personería jurídica*) and some pledgeable assets, they will be treated with the respect that is usually denied the single, virtually landless farmer. Thus the dream they were pursuing in 1975 may yet come true, after a long detour and "with different means."

The story is edifying, but could it have happened without that first step, the failed attempt to seize the land? The coop members certainly perceived a connection between their first collective action and its failure, on the one hand, and the fishing cooperative and its success, on the other.

The link between these two so dissimilar parts of the story can be interpreted at different levels. From one perspective, one may argue that the takeover of land is a daring act with revolutionary potential, whereas, in comparison, the "taking" of the sea through cooperatively operated fishing boats seems a tame entrepreneurial initiative. From this point of view, the taking of the land looms as far more arduous and demanding than the taking of (or to) the sea. One might then interpret the sequence from attempted land takeover to fishing cooperative as a renunciation of former goals, an acceptance of the existing order, and a settling down within it.

Yet, a good argument can be made for the opposite conclusion. The most obvious, simple, elementary collective action for *minifundista* peasants surrounded by partially idle *latifundios* is to seize as a group some of the idle land by a one-time act. The formation of a fishing cooperative requires, in contrast, a complex process of working out rules and procedures and of acquiring new knowledge and collaborative habits. From this perspective, the takeover of land seems rather simplistic, while setting out to sea looks far more complex and, in its own way, more hazardous.

There is some truth in both conceptions, and both help explain what happened. Once the historic moment when land reform was a real possibility in northern Colombia had passed, people obviously resigned themselves and looked in other, less overtly subversive, directions. But the experience of the attempted land takeover was also a real stepping stone to the fishing cooperative in the usual sense of stepping *up* rather than down. Having cooperated in the takeover of land, the Cristo Rey peasants had practiced cooperation at the most rudimentary level; having thus dispelled mutual distrust, forged a community, and—perhaps most important—created a *vision of change*, they were now ready for joint endeavors that required much greater sophistication and persistence.

This sort of dynamic can account for the numerous other cases where early participation in public action of one kind leads later to involvements in collective endeavors of a very different nature. In Colombia's Cauca Valley we had long sessions with two groups of peasant leaders that organize cooperatives and other kinds of community efforts throughout the Valley. They are known as *Muchachos de Buga*—the "Buga boys"—and the *Líderes de Tuluá*—the "leaders from Tuluá." Buga and Tuluá are towns north of Cali right in the valley, but we first met members of both of these groups in a consumer cooperative in Versalles, a provincial center in the Western Cordillera adjoining the valley. The *Líderes de Tuluá* are men in their fifties and sixties who are now primarily con-

Tuluá, Cauca Valley, Colombia: *Lideres de Tuluá* in cooperative warehouse office.

cerned —when they don't work their own farms—with building up a network of consumer and producer cooperatives. These cooperatives now have a central warehouse in Tuluá, the geographical center of the Valley. Seeing the gleaming warehouse and its offices full of shiny furniture, one would never suspect it is run by poor peasants who have been actively involved with the successive experiments in social change and reform in Colombia during the past twenty-five years. They all started with the *Acción Comunal* (community action programs) which mobilized people in the smaller towns and villages for cooperative construction of urgent public works in the early 1960s, and later participated in efforts at more active implementation of land reform in the late 1960s and early 1970s.[10]

[10] The self-told life histories of the principal figures of the group are in Robert Wasserstrom, *If We Didn't Argue It Wouldn't Be a Meeting: Oral Histories of Social Change in Latin America and the Caribbean* (to be published), Chapter 3.

Tuluá: consumer store at cooperative warehouse.

The story of the *Muchachos de Buga* is a bit different. This group of about ten younger men—now in their early thirties—were selected in their late teens to attend an experimental educational program at Buga (Department of Valle) which was called the *Academia Mayor Campesina*. The program's founder and director was a strong-minded Jesuit priest who set out to form peasant leaders able to help improve the communities to which they were expected to return upon graduation. The *Muchachos*—a group of ten to twelve graduates—were so fired by their educational experience and the then favorable prospects for substantial changes in Colombia's agrarian structure, that they decided to stay together as a group and to work actively for change, not only in their own communities, but wherever they might be helpful. They participated, during the early 1970s, in a few land invasions that were largely unsuccessful.

By the middle of the decade the group had changed; now they looked out for other kinds of opportunities to "better the condition" of the people in Colombia's villages. They became,

Buga, Cauca Valley, Colombia: *Muchachos de Buga* on their farm.

in fact, a private group of extension agents and called themselves *Cooperativa de Producción Agropecuaria* or COOPROAGRO. But they practiced agricultural extension with a difference: they imparted not only improved agricultural techniques, but also advice on how to form cooperatives and other community organizations, how to lobby for needed public improvements, how to use the courts to defend campesinos' rights, and so on. Individual members of COOPROAGRO went to work for various local groups interested in *promoción social*, but were at the same time intent on maintaining their own organization. In this endeavor, they were aided by a grant from the IAF which enabled them to acquire a dairy farm near Buga as an income-producing asset for the group. For the time being, however, the farm functions mainly as a temporary haven for any *muchacho* who is out of work. The possibility of staying at the farm for a limited period strengthens the independence of any individual member of the group working as an ''extension agent'': he knows that he does not need to fear unduly the consequences of speaking out (of using ''voice'') in his job,

GETTING AHEAD COLLECTIVELY

since quitting or being fired (deciding or having to "exit") is an eventuality of last resort that is not "the end of the world."

The consistency with which our Principle of Conservation and Mutation of Social Energy could be observed in Colombia borders on the monotonous. How could I expect to find it in operation once again when visiting a hammock-weavers' co-operative in Morroa, in the Atlantic Coast Department of

Morroa, Caribbean coast, Colombia; Ana Tomosa Padilla, Vice President of the hammock weavers cooperative.

Morroa: finishing a hammock.

Sucre? The cooperative was composed entirely, well almost entirely, of women weavers who had set up their enterprise with some guidance from the Bogotá-based Museum of Popular Arts and Traditions (*Museo de Artes y Tradiciones Populares*). The Museum is a remarkably effective organization that is providing various types of assistance to the practitioners of traditional handicrafts in the country without forcing craftsmen into mass production. On the contrary, the organization is attempting to revitalize the genuine traditions of individual workmanship (see also below, Chapter 6).

We visited the almost completed locale of the cooperative on the much-traveled Medellín-Cartagena highway. In part a gift of the Inter-American Foundation, it was soon to house the cooperative's offices as well as a sales outlet. There we were introduced to many members of the coop, and all of its leaders were waiting for us. They were all women and active weavers except for the president, a highly verbal *man* in his early forties who was, somewhat incongruously, the chief person to speak for the group. It was explained to us that a man was needed to deal with the authorities and banks in this somewhat backward Colombian department; perhaps also, he owed his position to the fact that many of these women weavers had recently been swindled by one of their own companions who had talked them into some fraudulent "cooperative" arrangement.

However that may be, my curiosity about the motivation of this man was aroused. I engaged him in a one-to-one conversation as we walked from the highway to the village where we were to view the handsome looms of some of the coop members. Within the first three minutes of our conversation, he told me that in the early seventies he had actively participated in some of the land seizures in the department and that, ever since that heady, if largely unsuccessful, experience, he had wanted to involve himself again in "doing something for the community!"

EXTENSIONS OF THE PRINCIPLE

Other instances of our principle in operation could be cited: from the leadership of the *pueblo joven*, El Rescate, in Lima, to the recent revival of some agricultural cooperatives in the Llanquíhue province of southern Chile. But perhaps it is of greater interest to draw some lessons and to attempt a more general formulation.

First of all, I must relate the principle to an old point of mine. I have often complained about the excessive and, I have come to think, highly damaging tendency of Latin Americans to categorize most of their experiences in social and political reform—or for that matter in economic development—as utter failures. This failure complex, or *fracasomania*, may itself lead to real failures, or so it has seemed to me. It can now be seen that—not surprisingly—the Principle of Conservation and Mutation of Social Energy fits right into my campaign against the failure complex. As long as the operation of the principle is not perceived, it will seem as though a social movement that has not achieved its preordained objective, such as the movement for agrarian reform in Colombia, is an unqualified failure. But this judgment must be altered, at least in part, once it is realized that the social energies that were aroused in the course of that movement did not pass from the scene even though the movement itself did. These energies remained, as it were, in *storage*[11] for a while, but were available to fuel later, perhaps very different, movements. In a real sense, the original movement must therefore be credited with whatever advances or successes were achieved by those subsequent movements: no longer can it be considered a *total* failure.

Now I return once more, for comparative purposes, to the fishing cooperative of Cristo Rey. It came into being through the sense of comradeship and community, the dispelling of isolation and original mutual distrust (almost in the sense of original sin), that resulted from the common action taken many years before. That action, though, had failed, and failure is dispiriting. What must have happened then, is that the positive experience of community and solidarity outweighed the impact of failure which would ordinarily make for withdrawal from collective action. Later we came across situations where the initial phase of getting together was not attended by failure. In Bogotá we visited an organization that is supplying financial assistance to worker-managed enterprises. Among them are some firms, primarily in clothing and footwear, that are staffed and managed predominantly or exclusively by women. These firms invariably originate, so we were told, in some *other* common activity where the women have gotten to know and like each other. Most frequently, the women met in courses given by SENA, the vocational training agency of the Colombian government. Upon graduating from the course—no failure here—they decided to set up an enterprise of their own rather than look for work as employees of existing firms.

The sequence involved is not too dissimilar from the ones discussed earlier. The common experience of the land invasion at Cristo Rey which led to other, more complex forms of cooperation, is replaced by the common experience of taking a course together and getting to know and like each other. On the one hand, the ties formed in this fashion are likely to be less strong than in the Cristo Rey case; on the other, this group did not have to pass through dispiriting initial failure to come together in a joint endeavor. As an economist I had expected

---

[11] I take this metaphor from Wolf Lepenies who has used it to very good effect in a different context. See his ''Transformation and Storage of Scientific Traditions in Literature,'' in Leonard Schulze and Walter Wetzels, *Literature and History* (Lanham, N.Y.: University Press of America, 1983), pp. 37–63.

GETTING AHEAD COLLECTIVELY

that the need to mobilize a minimal amount of capital would be at the root of at least some of the cooperative, worker-managed enterprises. But it turned out that a more fundamental need is, once again, some experience dispelling isolation and mutual distrust.

Chapter Five

Intangible Benefits and Costs of Cooperatives

A large number of the grassroots development projects we visited were cooperatives of one kind or another. We met with large and small coops, with consumer, producer and construction coops, with rural and urban coops, and finally with federations of coops known also as second-level coops. A first approximation to the evaluation of coop performance is of course the financial success or failure of these organizations. With their financial health being often precarious and with their ability to coexist in an individualistic market society with purely profit-oriented firms being frequently in doubt, cooperatives tend to be judged by their financial record alone. But just as the social and political effects of capitalism must be considered in any overall evaluation of that mode of production, so do we need to know something about the non-monetary costs and benefits of coops for any comprehensive appraisal of their role. It turns out, moreover, that these non-monetary or intangible effects are frequently crucial to the understanding of their performance in the marketplace.

BENEFITS (WITH A STORY FROM PERU'S ALTIPLANO)

Some of these benefits of coops have already been noted in connection with the sequences that were discussed in the first two chapters. In Chapter 1, for example, it was shown how

the establishment of cooperatives provides powerful incentives
toward literacy and other forms of education for members of
the coops and particularly, of course, for those who manage
coop activities. In Chapter 2, certain cooperative activities, originally undertaken strictly to improve the private economic position of members (sewing lessons, mutual guaranteeing of *tricicleros'* installment debt), were seen to lead to constructive
involvement in public affairs and to public advocacy.

There are other, more general benefits of coops to which it
is impossible to attach a monetary value. One is, no doubt, the
establishment and strengthening of ties of friendship and part-
nership among members, perhaps best expressed by the statement of a *triciclero* from Santo Domingo: ''[Before our asso-
ciation] I saw him around, but I didn't *know* him'' as well as
by that of a Cristo Rey fisherman: ''We have learned how to
discuss.'' No doubt, these benefits will at times have a negative
value as the conflicts that inevitably arise will lead to personal
enmities and to clique formation.

At an even more general level, the formation of a cooperative
is one of those human activities that bring their own reward.
For many groups, the fact of joining forces, be it even for a
modest purpose, such as the setting up of a cooperative consumer store, has a great deal of symbolic value. It is an act of
self-affirmation that fills people with pride and may even be
felt as a beginning of liberation, particularly by long-suffering
and long-oppressed groups. This sort of intangible benefit of
cooperative action was present in a number of situations, but
was perhaps most strongly evident in the Peruvian highlands.
Here several consumer stores, financed by the IAF, had been
set up by various communities of Aymara-speaking Indians
around Pilcuyo, near the town of Ilave which is on the Puno-
La Paz highway along Lake Titicaca, not far from Puno. In the
course of a long day, we visited five or six of these consumer
stores. They were always located at the center of communities—as the whole altiplano in that area is very densely settled
by small-holding peasants, this merely means that the density
at those points was somewhat higher than average—with an
open meeting space next to them, and usually a chapel and a
flagpole also nearby. The stores occupied a corner of newly
and jointly built, fairly spacious community houses. After having looked at the often quite rudimentary stock of merchandise, we held meetings right there with large groups of coop

Pilcuyo, Peru (near Lake Titicaca): cooperative members in front of warehouse and own truck.

members, and inquired about the benefits of the coop. The usual ones were mentioned, such as lower prices for some items and the saving of time—the peasants could now obtain some essential items in their village when previously they had to travel, usually on foot, all the way to Ilave.

But we sensed that this was not the whole story. Now a further point frequently made in favor of the stores was the relief from suspicion of being cheated by the city merchants duly equipped with ''fixed'' scales and other sharp ways of swindling the poor and ignorant rural folk. Here we are getting close to the more general intangible benefit mentioned earlier. For the Aymara-speaking Indians, the store is akin to a declaration of emancipation from the mestizo, Spanish-speaking merchants who are for them very much part of a system that has oppressed and exploited them for centuries. In a more positive view, the store is a symbol of the community's ability to undertake a joint effort and of its aspiration to ''better its condition'' as a solidarity group. The connection between the store and these broader objectives and benefits finds its visual

GETTING AHEAD COLLECTIVELY

and spatial expression in the location of the store in the center of the village and in the way in which the building of the store has served as the pretext for erecting a community meeting house as an annex, as it were, to the store.

This sort of symbolic value of the cooperative consumer store is also present in other peasant communities, even though cleavages between country and city may not be as deep as on the Peruvian altiplano. The poor peasant's most frequent contacts with the outside world are the neighboring landlords who may employ him as a day laborer at certain times of the year *and* the town merchants who purchase his excess produce or some of the animals he raises and where he buys in turn the staples and agricultural imports he needs as well as all those modern "trinkets and baubles" (Adam Smith), from bicycles to radios and televisions. Just as the *minifundista's* relation with the landlord makes for periodic conflict, so do the dealings with the town merchants generate a desire to "manage by oneself" and to set up a peasant cooperative that will "cut out" the middlemen, the "monopolists" as they were routinely called in Colombia and the Dominican Republic. In many ways, the setting up of a cooperative is the equivalent of achieving land reform and *is felt to be so* by the peasants. To a visiting outsider, these stores often seem unsubstantial ventures whose principal advertised function, that of bringing prices down for the articles farmers buy and of raising prices for the items farmers sell, is not likely to be spectacularly successful. After all, retailing is an economic activity, entry into which is fairly easy and which for that reason tends to be overcrowded in the service-intensive economies of Latin America. Even if prices are kept artificially high in small, isolated communities as a result of "conspiracies" among the local merchants, a coop will be able to offer lower prices on consumer goods and agricultural imports than the merchants only for a short time, since the merchants will be able to respond by lowering their prices and shaving their excess profits. This is indeed what happens frequently[12] and in that case the major economic benefit of the coop for the member is likely to be of rather short duration. If coops endure after this initial positive

[12] See Judith Tendler, *What to Think About Cooperatives: A Guide From Bolivia* (The Inter-American Foundation, 1983, processed), Chapter 6.

experience has petered out and prices quoted by the coop and the merchants have become quite comparable, it is precisely because of the symbolic value they have for their members.

There is something rather complex about this symbolic, non-monetary benefit. It is present only as long as the coop itself is able to function as a viable enterprise, a going concern. In other words, the intangible benefits (pride, self-confidence, feeling of liberation, etc.) enhance the purely monetary benefits of the coop, but they do not make up for the monetary losses for the simple reason that they do not survive such losses. When the coop is in financial trouble for any reason (such as loss of patronage, poor management, or corruption), the intangible benefits are also likely to turn into losses as pride is being hurt, self-confidence is being impaired, and the hopes for liberation are once again being dashed. It appears that these intangible benefits of coops are essentially fair-weather friends; more precisely, they are in the nature of those warts that make a person more lovable when she or he is loved and more unattractive once love gives way to indifference or worse.

With the non-monetary, intangible effects of coops being fickle in this way, it is not surprising that the fortunes of coops can turn rather rapidly. When the coop prospers its good fortune is reinforced by the intangible benefits it generates on top of the tangible ones. Loyalty to the coop will be strong among members, making for even more successful operation. Once the coop falters, however, the intangible benefits turn into losses and the demoralization over the various hopes that have gone sour will induce disloyalty among the members along with, perhaps, corrupt behavior among the staff. The intangible benefits (or losses) thus have an important impact on the tangible ones, compounding rather than offsetting them. As a result of this cumulative effect, one might expect coops to be in either excellent or terrible shape, more so than private business. For whatever it is worth, our sample of coop stores confirms this deduction.

There is a further advantage of the consumer and agricultural input cooperative store: its ready availability as a cooperative device. Like the strike for workers, the consumer store holds a privileged place in the repertoire of conceivable collective actions on the part of peasants living in remote rural surroundings. When such people come to the point where they want to join in a common enterprise, the consumer store always looms as a beckoning possibility, something that can be tried out if only you can get hold of the needed working capital and of an appropriate locale. The consumer store is thus an excellent device for *doing something* right away once the desire for cooperative action has arisen. It may not be the most useful or productive thing to do, but its great advantage is that it serves as a temporary outlet for the urge to cooperate. In the process, people are brought together and talk to each other about the problems of the community, with the result that they become aware of those other more useful and productive, but also more ambitious and difficult, ventures that might be undertaken next. In this sense, the consumer store can have yet another intangible benefit: it leads to heightened interaction among the cooperating members who will now explore new forms of cooperative action. In the process, some of the more fundamental problems of the community will be tackled.

The best illustration for this sequence is supplied again by the Pilcuyo communities of Aymara-speaking Indians. Having established their consumer stores and meeting places, these communities, impelled also by the punishing drought of 1983

Pilcuyo: family scene.

that ruined their potato crop, soon came up with something far more ambitious and difficult to organize than consumer stores: a plan for increasing the capacity of the altiplano peasants to fatten cattle and thereby to improve their cash earnings so they will not be so dependent for their livelihood on the vagaries of the potato crop. At present the usual practice is for each peasant family to buy a cow, to fatten it up, and then to sell it. Because the individual lots owned by the peasants are so small, the cow is tethered. As in much of India, its pasture, such as the totora grass that grows in the shallow waters of Lake Titicaca, is brought to it in cut form. Again as in India, the cow supplies the household not only with milk but also with cooking fuel, through its droppings. But the most important contribution of the operation is the net profit realized through resale of the cow once it is fattened up. The resulting cash income permits the peasant family to supplement their homegrown subsistence with items, such as rice and sugar, that are bought in the marketplace.

In 1982–83, an exceptionally severe drought hit the Southern

Pilcuyo: milking tethered cow.

GETTING AHEAD COLLECTIVELY

Peruvian highlands near Lake Titicaca and the Pilcuyo communities faced near-famine conditions as the potato crop failed. In response, the communities which had just recently established their consumer cooperatives, came up with an entirely new scheme for increasing everyone's cash earnings. A fund was to be set up from which loans would be made available to a fraction of the peasant families for the purpose of buying an additional cow; upon repayment of the loans by the first beneficiaries, the fund would be refilled and it would be enabled to make similar loans to a second set of members; and so on until everyone would have two cows instead of one. A problem arose in the course of elaborating the plan and discussing it with possible funding agencies such as the IAF: how would one select the lucky winners who would be the first ones to benefit from the scheme? The plan as presented by the cooperative called for the leaders of the cooperative to be the first beneficiaries, but this solution could be (and was) criticized as self-serving by others.

No matter how this particular problem is resolved, it became clear that the leaders of the cooperative had come up with a scheme that, if successful, would make a more substantial contribution to the bettering of their members' condition than the consumer stores they had previously sponsored could ever hope to make. At the same time, the latter had clearly been an essential steppingstone to the elaboration of the new scheme. Any success of the second stage must thus be ascribed in part to the first stage of the cooperative program.[13]

The Pilcuyo sequence which, incidentally, had close parallels elsewhere among our projects, spells out an effective reply to one frequently voiced "radical" criticism of cooperatives: that cooperatives divert energies for social change into innocuous channels when these energies could otherwise produce far-reaching "structural transformation." Whereas cooperatives could surely on occasion have this diversionary effect, the Pilcuyo example shows that the opposite sequence is just as con-

[13] In her study of Bolivian cooperatives, Judith Tendler makes a related point. Just as the coop, so does the funding agency go through a learning process and it cannot therefore be very inquisitive and demanding when it first decides to assist a grassroots organization. "Only the second time around will the donor be able to learn how the socio-economic environment of a particular coop interacts with the nature of the tasks it undertakes." Tendler, *op. cit.*, p. 106.

ceivable: first, a "harmless" cooperative comes into being, but the ensuing discussions and deliberations among its members lead in due course to more ambitious projects and actions for change.

The sequence noted here—from the "harmless" consumer store, the "easy play" in the repertoire of collective action, to a more ambitious cooperative project—is in some sense the opposite of the one described in the last chapter in connection with the Principle of Conservation and Mutation of Social Energy. There people formed cooperatives *after* having undertaken far more daring collective actions such as land occupations. Actually, the two sequences can occur back to back and did so in the case of the Versalles cooperative in Colombia's Cauca Valley (see Chapter 4): here the leaders of the cooperative, essentially a consumer, agricultural input and marketing store, had been through many more militant battles before, together and separately; then, once they were involved in several cooperative stores, they developed ideas for more ambitious ventures, such as the establishment of a Cauca-Valley-wide network of stores, complete with trucks and a central warehouse in Tuluá.

DIGRESSION: SPORT AND SOCIAL CHANGE

I turn briefly to a topic related to the point just made about cooperatives: the effect of *sport* on social change. Here also, the naïve left-wing, somewhat conspiratorial view has long been that sport serves to "catch" all kinds of collective energies and emotions which, differently channelled, would have served to redress any number of social injustices. Yet again, the evidence we have gathered points in the opposite direction: a number of our most activist "social promoters" have stressed the importance of sport (soccer) in their life experiences. In the small towns of Colombia, for example, to play soccer on weekends often means a decision not to spend all one's time hanging out at the local bar. The planning and joint construction of a soccer field was one of the most popular tasks for the community action groups in the 1960s, and successful completion frequently led to other, more difficult projects being under-

Morroa: boys playing stickball.

taken. For youngsters growing up in the countryside, playing soccer is a means of breaking out of the isolation of family and rural life, of losing one's timidity and of becoming part of a wider community. In the words of two Colombians who are today among the leading organizers of cooperative action in the Cauca Valley:

Rogelio Giraldo: My father was very poor and after three years of school I had to help him work in the field. I worked with him until we were able to achieve some improvement in our economic conditions. When I was 14 or 15 years old I started to get together quite a bit with sports teams—playing soccer. This going out to other districts had the effect of my making connections with other persons. At the same time, I felt the need to look for ways of improving my education and training.

Delio de Jesus	
Cortez	
Ocampo:	I did not know a thing about these matters of organization; I did not know anything but how to work in the field—simply to work and to earn the wage they were giving us . . . I made one connection in the village: join a soccer team. But I was very shy, too much so. When a priest or person I considered to be educated was around I would't speak: I felt I shouldn't. When the priest came to our district I wouldn't get close to him. I didn't go to mass because he looked straight at me. These are problems of our people. But when I joined the soccer team I began to get a bit more social all around. That's where I met Don Eduardo Giraldo. One day he called out for me and said: "Compañero, why don't you come to a meeting I am going to?" Well I didn't really feel like going to the meeting, but he insisted: He even took me there himself and introduced me to Don Pedro and others. And they took me to a course in human promotion."[14]

In both these cases, soccer acts as the great socializer and initiates its adepts into the life of groups, organizations, and educational programs.

COSTS (WITH STORIES FROM
THE DOMINICAN REPUBLIC, URUGUAY AND PERU)

As has been noted in connection with Pilcuyo some of the intangible benefits of cooperatives change sign in certain circumstances and turn into losses. But the connection between intangible benefits and intangible costs can be more intimate: instead of arising in a temporal sequence, intangible costs can arise simultaneously with the benefits, being simply the other side of the same coin.

Take what was earlier described as the symbolic value of the cooperative consumer store, such as the pride and feeling

[14] Quoted from Wasserstrom, *op. cit.*, Chapter 3, pp. 9 and 45.

of liberation from the ''monopolists'' that comes with the opening of the store: this is the positive aspect of the affair. But there is a negative one: to be in good standing, members of the cooperative are expected to make their purchases in the cooperative store and to deliver their own marketable production to the cooperative rather than to local merchants. This obligation implies a certain loss of freedom for the members, however much they may have complained before about being exploited by the private traders. The loss consists not only in the impossibility, under the new circumstances, of cursing the ''monopolists'' and of blaming them for one's (perhaps not radically changed) plight; there is a real loss of choice, especially with respect to the selling of the farmer's own produce. Previously he was able to haggle with various potential buyers and then to pick and choose among them. Once the cooperative store is established, all of this maneuvering is a thing of the past and the member is supposed to bring whatever he has to sell straight to the coop without looking left or right. When prices paid by the coop are truly more advantageous than those paid by private traders this obligation is evidently not burdensome. But after the initial phase (see above), the private traders' prices tend to be competitive with those posted by the coop and in this case the member is frequently in a bit of a quandary.

The extent to which this problem arose differed greatly from case to case. We encountered it first in the Dominican Republic, in a cooperative of furniture makers in Santo Domingo. This cooperative had received a grant from the IAF for the purpose of making loans to members wishing to expand—or to initiate in the case of new members—their operations. We were commenting on the fine rocking chairs—a ''must'' item in every Dominican household—crowded together in the administrative headquarters of the cooperative which also serves as a salesroom, and a discussion soon broke out precisely about this point: are the members of the cooperative, the recipients of the grant, morally obliged to bring their whole production to this store? All agreed that specially commissioned items could be excepted, but for the rest members had very different conceptions about their obligations to sell all of their output through the coop store. Some of the members with special contracts and marketing skills were understandably loath to give them up, whereas others felt that such an attitude bespoke a lack of

Santo Domingo, Dominican Republic: a member of the cooperative sanding a door.

''conscientization''—using, somewhat to our surprise, this neologism coined by the Brazilian educator Paulo Freire that has caught on so widely in Latin America.

The takeover, by the cooperative, of the merchandising function can come to the producer either as a relief or a deprivation (and sometimes as a mixture of the two). Uruguay supplied us with illustrations for these two contrasting possibilities. At one end of the spectrum, there is the already mentioned dairy cooperative in Durazno whose truck picks up the members' milk production every day and delivers it to the new pasteurization plant. Previously every milk producer had to sell his own milk as best he could, usually by taking it on a horse-drawn cart into the town of Durazno. As noted earlier, this meant one and sometimes two daily trips for the farmer—a quite considerable time loss. Thus the new arrangement is widely felt as a considerable relief from a burdensome routine and menial task.

A very different situation is that of the wool producer who faces the question whether to sell his wool through private

GETTING AHEAD COLLECTIVELY

Santo Domingo:
reupholstering
furniture in the street.

channels or to the nationwide wool growers' cooperative *Central Lanera Uruguaya* (CLU). This cooperative works through the rural development societies (*Sociedades de Fomento Rural*) which are loose cooperatives functioning at the local level all over the country. Some of these societies are fairly perfunctory whereas others provide a wide variety of services, from the supply and manufacture of agricultural inputs to the processing of grains, milk, etc. With the exception of one or two provinces all of these societies function as reception centers for wool on behalf of the Montevideo-based CLU.

The CLU was established in the mid-sixties when, as a result of wide fluctuations in wool prices, the wool trade in Uruguay was in a serious crisis. As many private traders went broke, local growers frequently were not paid for already delivered wool or had to suffer serious delays and heavy discounts. The CLU was set up primarily to provide wool growers with an alternative, less risky sales outlet. Instead of buying the wool outright at a price leaving an estimated profit margin for sale in the world market, the CLU estimates the world price and pays the farmer 30% of that price upon his commitment, during the winter season, to sell his crop to CLU, and another 40% in late spring (October–November) upon delivery. The final settlement takes place several months later after the wool has actually been sold in world markets. At that point the *average* price received for each quality of wool is established and

Uruguay: sheep waiting to be sheared.

GETTING AHEAD COLLECTIVELY

Shearing sheep.

the farmer receives an additional payment, with due allowance
for the services rendered by CLU in connection with classifi-
cation, processing, packing, etc.

The wool cooperative has grown into a substantial organization. Its operation accounts for approximately 10% of Uruguay's annual wool crop, it is the fifth to sixth largest exporter
and its new, IAF-financed wool reception and processing center, just outside of Montevideo, is an impressive structure, both
beautiful and functional. In short, the organization is a success.

Given the excellent facilities of the CLU and its eminently
fair method of pricing and the credit element implicit in its
terms of payment, I was actually surprised that the CLU was
not doing still better. Why would its share of the national wool
crop not be higher? Moreover, it appeared from the organization's statistics that the rate of turnover among the wool growers delivering their wool to the CLU was surprisingly high. As
many as 25% to 33% of the growers who had used the CLU in
one year would turn to private traders the next; their places
were taken by others who would shift in the opposite direction

from private trade to CLU. What were the reasons for this fickleness?

One possible reason was suggested by our discussion with the directors of the CLU (who are all woolgrowers themselves). Unlike the dairy farmer who, prior to the establishment of the pasteurization plant, had to make *daily* trips to market his milk, the wool grower, who often leads an isolated life on his farm

Packing sheared wool (inside of bag there is a man packing down wool).

GETTING AHEAD COLLECTIVELY

in the countryside, shears his flock *once a year* and then sets out for a nearby town to sell the crop. There he will either "deliver" it to the CLU in the local *sociedad de fomento rural* or "sell" it to a private trader. The two operations have a very different cultural content. In the case of the "delivery" the sheep farmer will be paid up to 70% of the already firmly-set CLU-estimated price for the wool or 40% if he has taken an advance; the final settlement will be known only months later. The "sale," on the other hand, carries with it a great deal of drama and entertainment value. There is not only the uncertainty, appealing to some "risk-lovers," about the outcome of the bargaining process. The sale of a yearly wool crop of any size at all involves a great deal of foreplay: the grower is greeted as he comes into town, he is invited for drinks at the local bars, he is complimented about the beautiful quality of his wool *(qué linda su lana!)*—in short, for this one day he is treated by the potential buyers as a most desirable party and enjoys himself thoroughly in the process. No wonder many sheep farmers, especially perhaps those of medium size (the big growers often have direct ties to the private export houses), are not ready to exchange this sort of excitement for the quiet and prosaic ways of the CLU and quite a few of those who deal with the CLU desert it every once in a while in order to experience once again the thrills of negotiating their crop in the open market.

Such, then, are some of the intangible losses or costs of cooperative action. As noted in connection with the furniture makers of Santo Domingo, it involves not only a loss of "fun" that might not be considered serious by those exclusively concerned with income maximization. The counterpart of this loss of fun is the loss or atrophy of real bargaining and entrepreneurial skills, as a result of non-use of these skills over a prolonged period, while the cooperative takes over the functions that require, call forth, and exercise those skills.

The intangible loss we have been dealing with is, in a sense, a by-product of the very purpose and alleged principal benefit of the cooperative. To the extent that a coop achieves its objective of saving the farmer from exploitation by the middleman, it will sever the previous contacts between these two actors. But this means that the farmer will no longer use whatever skill he may have previously developed on his own in dealing with the middleman.

At this point, however, it is useful to show, by another example, that things are not quite so neat and that the loss of members' entrepreneurial abilities is not an inevitable by-product of cooperatives. We came across at least one situation where such abilities were fostered rather than restrained or suppressed by the coop. This is the case of the agricultural cooperative Tupac Amaru, located 60 miles south of Lima on the Pacific Coast. Here some 50 workers, many of them former

Cooperative Tupac Amaru, south of Lima, Peru: preparing grape vine for next harvest.

GETTING AHEAD COLLECTIVELY

plantation laborers, cultivate jointly 120 hectares of irrigated land. The tasty "Italia" grapes are one of the principal cash crops. Upon being picked the grapes are gone over carefully and the less perfect ones are cut off to be sold to distilleries producing pisco, the famous Peruvian spirit. The rest are then sold as table grapes. The cooperative sells the grapes for pisco to the distilleries, but it has not taken over the trading function for the table grapes. Rather, it permits every member to buy from it, at a basic price, as many kilograms of table grapes as he or she asks for. The member or someone in his family is then expected to do his own merchandising, either in nearby towns and beaches or by taking a car or bus to Lima. How much the individual members make by way of profit in the process is strictly their own business.

This is a cooperative, it should be noted, with a highly developed collective work structure, where members have no private plots of their own—they engage jointly in commercial agriculture on a full-time basis. But, in a pragmatic spirit, it was no doubt felt that the members could do best for themselves by the capillary distribution network that would come into being as each member marketed his own bunch of grapes. Perhaps the furniture makers of Santo Domingo could learn from them!

This section holds a lesson also for the organizations extending financial aid to cooperatives: "the more the better" does not necessarily hold for cooperative action. Since there is a cost to that action it may be well to question certain peripheral components of cooperative ventures: in some of these the costs of cooperative organization may outweigh the benefits and to reorganize them on a non-cooperative basis may in the end strengthen the cooperative core of the venture.

Chapter Six

Organizations Involved in Social Activism

In the course of our trip through six Latin American countries, we visited some forty-five "grassroots" projects, from six to nine per country. In the preceding, highly selective account, only about half this number have been specifically drawn upon to illustrate various points, but the others contributed in many ways to the picture I have tried to draw here. I now turn to another type of organization that has already been mentioned in passing: the groups which have grown up all over Latin America with the purpose of helping low-income people to better their condition through self-help, mutual help, and articulation of their demands and grievances. The presence of these groups on the social stage is an important factor in the development of many grassroots actions; their social and political impact shall be noted in the next and final chapter.

In describing these groups the first problem one meets is that of referring to them by a proper generic name. I rather dislike the terms "intermediary" or "broker" organizations, which have become fairly current within the Inter-American Foundation and perhaps also among other international donors to grassroots activities. Quite apart from the somewhat derogatory or condescending connotation of these terms, their implication is that the people forming these organizations have done so in order to act as some sort of "middlemen" making a tidy profit from their work.[15] While it is of course true that the Inter-American Foundation and other grassroots funding agencies often work closely with these groups to make contact with the "real" grassroots, the men and women of these organizations do not at all think of themselves as having "set up in business" to serve as intermediaries between international donors and grassroots recipients. All of these entities were established in response to pressing social, political, and economic problems in their own countries and out of the new perception, arising in the past fifteen years or so, that it was possible to do something about these problems at the local level regardless of whatever large-scale "structural" changes were needed or likely to happen at the national level. In Latin America, the people undertaking these tasks are usually referred to as *promotores* doing *promoción social* (similar to the French *animateur* and *animation sociale*), but unfortunately the corresponding English words "promoter" and "promotion" also carry derogatory meanings, just like "broker." Although not fully satisfactory, the term "social activist" is perhaps the most appropriate in English and I shall use it here, along with "social promotion."

An enormous variety of such social activist organizations have sprung up in Latin America. A good number are or were initially related to the Catholic Church or to some Protestant missionary activities, but others start out with quite diverse ideological or political moorings. In general, the initiators, directors and members of the activist teams have some university or professional education—they are architects, planners, medical doctors, social scientists, social workers, etc. But we have already come across exceptions to this rule: in Colombia we met with groups—the COOPROAGRO (*Muchachos de Buga*) and the *Lideres de Tuluá*—whose social roots lie in the very peasantry on whose behalf they have banded together.

With respect to size, the range is wide: it goes from large, well-staffed organizations, sometimes with a highly Establishment-leaning Board of Directors, to three-to-four person store-front operations. With respect to effectiveness our impression was that the range is of similar magnitude. Some

---

[15] Another term I rather dislike, this one primarily on esthetic grounds, is "facilitator."

organizations (not necessarily or not only the big ones) have by now accumulated considerable experience and sophistication, while others are somewhat uncertain of their mission and are not fully accepted by their "clients." Finally, some groups were specifically set up with the purpose of organizing grass-roots activities, while others took a turn in this direction much later in their existence. They may for example have devoted themselves to social science research for several years before being tempted to combine theory with practice and to engage in *promoción social*.[16]

To convey a feeling for the nature, functioning and diversity of such groups, a brief sketch of some of them and of their principal activities will be useful.

FOUR CASE STUDIES

Asociación para la Vivienda Económica (AVE), Córdoba, Argentina

This organization was founded by architects and engineers in the mid-sixties and was then part of the University of Córdoba. It became an independent legal entity in 1977 when the universities in Argentina had become the objects of "interventions" by the governing military. It consists today of some thirty professionals (including several graduate students): the architects are still in the key positions, but a number of sociologists, social workers and even an economist have been added to the staff. The basic ideology of the group is a progressive catholicism, with a strongly held belief that man can fully realize himself only as a member of a community.

The principal activity of AVE is the cooperative rehabilitation and rebuilding of slum housing and, more recently, the planning of very low-cost housing projects built collectively by the prospective owners. In carrying out these tasks AVE exhibits two characteristics that might be considered contradictory, but that actually coexist quite effectively. On the one hand, there is considerable concentration on technical matters, that

[16] I am not concerned here with the special kind of activity that aims at combining systematically research and action: "action research" or *investigación acción*.

is, upon innovation with respect to building materials and building techniques. A number of patents in these areas have been taken out. The architects and engineers of the group have in particular developed novel building methods and materials for people who work *jointly* on a house without having had much prior building experience.

The other characteristic of the group is in the opposite direction: it deemphasizes the house as the end-all of its activity or as the solution of poor people's problems. AVE's practice has led it "beyond housing" in three important respects:

(1) Housing is not always a high-priority need of poor people—they often do well enough building their own homes and need help primarily in other areas—for example, utilities and services. We have already met with the community at La Merced whose first priority was water supply and noted how AVE helped them get it.

(2) The other proposition that has become central to AVE's work is that low-cost housing should never be pursued as an end in itself. Rather, building or rebuilding should be so or-

La Merced: making windows with help of mold according to AVE instructions.

ganized that present or future homeowners become active members of a solidarity group through the *work* they jointly perform. This caring for group values and group integrity appeared also in other areas of AVE's work. In selecting future occupants for its new building projects, AVE attempts not to deprive existing *villas miserias* of their emergent leaders even though such persons may be eminently eligible. In this manner, the organization is aware of the danger that it might build up its own groups at the expense of weakening group cohesion elsewhere.

(3) Finally, AVE is attempting to develop, in all of its housing activities, new sources of employment for the members of its projects. Being primarily knowledgeable about the construction business, it has promoted cooperative workshops producing doors, windows and other housing components which it can then use in its own construction activities. The hope is, of course, that these workshops will eventually be able to go beyond this stage of "taking in each other's washings" and to find customers on the outside; and this is already occurring with regard to the most elaborate construction cooperative that has been set up under AVE's auspices.

The expertise of AVE in the low-cost cooperative housing field has attracted people concerned with related problems in other Argentine cities where AVE advisers are increasingly in demand. Financial assistance is forthcoming not only from the Inter-American Foundation, but from the Dutch CEBEMO group as well as from Argentina's official science and technology foundation (*Consejo de Investigaciones en Ciencias y Tecnologia*).

Museo de Artes y Tradiciones Populares, Bogotá, Colombia

The Association was formed in 1966 by a group of Colombians who lived in Bogotá, but maintained strong ties to their native regions. They shared a common interest in popular arts and handicrafts, and a concern for the problems faced by artisans. The members of this group were mostly women, working for the Association as volunteers. Similar groups at the regional level, closer to the local artisans, were also established. In the early years, the principal activity of the Association was the founding of the *Museo de Artes y Tradiciones Populares* in Bogotá and its installation in a prime location: a handsome colonial monastery in the old center of Bogotá, next to the Presidential Palace. The acquisition and thorough renovation of the building was a major undertaking; to see it through financially, the Association was able to enlist support from Bogotá high society and from the Government.

The guiding spirit of the operation was Cecilia Duque, a woman with training and experience in museum management and remarkably endowed with both energy and taste—always a rare combination. As Director of the Museum she then mounted a fine collection of handicraft objects, installed a series of anthropological exhibits, and set up a store with handicraft merchandise for sale (one of Bogotá's better restaurants with *típico* food also functions on the Museum's premises). But the Museum's principal assignment, so she felt, was not just to collect what there still was of genuine handicraft and popular art, but to maintain the traditions of Colombia's artisans

Cecilia Duque, Director of the Museum of Popular Arts and Traditions, Bogotá, Colombia (in cloister of colonial convent housing the Museum).

and to help revitalize them where they were in decline ("decline" included for the Museum those unfortunately not infrequent cases where well-intentioned attempts at "modernization" had increased the quantity of handicraft output, but at the cost of disastrous deterioration in quality).

Today the Museum has a small, but qualified and dedicated staff of artists, anthropologists and social workers who have developed close relationships with some of the finest groups of artisans in the country, often in quite remote places. One of these, Morroa with its hammock-weavers, has already figured in these pages (See Chapter 4) and I shall now relate another incident that took place during our visit there and that is revealing of the kind of work the Museum and its staff are carrying on.

We were accompanied by Colombia Vivas, a former social worker, now employed by the Museum. She had helped the weavers set up their new cooperative and the Inter-American Foundation had collaborated with her and the Museum in contributing funds enabling the coop to buy an initial supply of wool for the cooperators. We held an extended meeting with the hammock weavers in their new locale; toward the end of the meeting, we noticed a good number of young men peeking in and intently watching the proceedings from the doors and windows. They were the sons of the weavers, and eventually they were invited to join, particularly by Colombia. They did so after some hesitation.

A new discussion now started. These young men—most of them were just out of high school—complained about being left out of all this new exciting development taking place around them. Apparently their parents—and particularly their mothers—had managed to see them through a full high school education. In contrast to the mothers who looked generally worn and often sickly, the young men struck us as the picture of health, good looks and correct dress. But, as happens often, their education had alienated them from the traditions and values of their parents' work without preparing them adequately for alternate careers. They seemed to have no idea what to do with their lives and education or where to look for work. The coastal cities of Cartagena and Barranquilla are currently plagued by unemployment, and even in neighboring Venezuela the prospects for finding work as illegal immigrants are no longer promising.

Morroa: member of hammock weavers cooperative with her son.

Colombia Vivas seized on the occasion to ask the young men some hard questions: Why wouldn't they help their mothers with their work in some fashion? Why wouldn't they think about selling the hammocks by peddling them from house to house in nearby cities? Why wouldn't they have at least built some furniture for the new locale (we all had to sit on the floor)? And she invited them to a session the next day during which everyone's proposals would be welcome. Later, back in Bogotá, she reported that it had been a good meeting. The sons had come around to taking more of an interest in their mothers' business and to exploring new ways of distributing their beautiful products, and Colombia would explore how the Museum could be helpful.

When Cecilia Duque stated, in an early program announcement, that the Museum will focus on the artisan rather than on the handicraft product, she did not perhaps realize to what extent it would become involved in the social and human problems of the groups with which it works.

*Asociación de Promoción
y Desarrollo Social* (APDES),
Comas (Lima), Peru

I am selecting this organization as an example of quite small and precarious groups of professionals that start out with the general idea of doing *something* for low-income communities without any very clear initial idea what that might be and how to go about it. APDES, and acronym standing grandly for *Asociación de Promoción y Desarrollo Social* (Association for Social Promotion and Development), works out of the most rudimentary office in a typical *pueblo joven*. It consists of four or five young men in their twenties or early thirties who were brought up in Comas (See Chapter 2), and kept in touch while attending different universities in Lima—San Marcos, Federico Villareal, and the National Engineering University. They graduated in accounting, economics, and industrial engineering. After a few years in sundry employments they decided to work together for their own community which they had never really left, having maintained their homes there. The immediate cause of their decision was the return of democracy and free voting to Peru after a decade of military government and, more specifically, the establishment in Comas of a municipal government which they thought would be receptive to the kind of part research, part promotional work they were contemplating. They told us that they had never taken an active part in student politics—to them this activity, especially on the part of "Comas boys," smacked of the desire to leave one's own community behind by involving oneself in *national* politics.

The Inter-American Foundation decided to help this fledgling group by financing surveys and studies to be carried out in agreement with the municipality, but under the responsibility of APDES, in public administration, public health, and employment generation.

We became acquainted mostly with APDES's work in employment generation by visiting some of the workshops installed under this program: a bakery and a small factory of school uniforms. The latter visit turned out to be particularly interesting, for here we met with the previously mentioned Women's Academy. During the three-month vacation period at the beginning of the calendar year, the women who normally work as teachers there had decided to keep busy by manufacturing uniforms to be sold at rock bottom prices; the commercial cost of this item makes it impossible for many Comas parents to send their children to school. The overt role of APDES in these various ventures is to contribute entrepreneurial ideas and assistance in accounting and marketing, but it also serves as an informal point of contact with, and entry into, Comas for outside social activist groups. Thus APDES had developed a good working relationship with the group that had originally supplied the teachers to the Women's Academy and then had partially withdrawn as the Comas women became able to take over. This group, which calls itself the *Centro de Estudios Sociales y Publicaciones*, functions in central Lima, miles away from Comas, is staffed by middle-class men and women, has a primary interest in adult education, and uses APDES as a means of access to various Comas communities.

The Comas group resembles the COOPROAGRO or *Muchachos de Buga* group in Colombia in that it also grew out of the community itself. Its members returned to set up APDES in Comas after a short detour via university and professional experience, just as the *Muchachos de Buga* who were born as farmers formed a group to encourage cooperative and other self-help efforts of farmers after an even shorter detour via the *Academia Mayor Campesina*. In both cases the rapport of the activists with the grassroots "clients" was predictably easy. On the other hand, the absence of backing by a solid sponsoring organization, such as a church, a party, or a movement, and the lack of financial reserves usually available to middle class undertakings made one wonder about the durability of these enterprises. In both cases, the financial support of the Foundation was, for this reason, particularly essential.

Instituto de Promoción Económico-Social del Uruguay (IPRU), Montevideo, Uruguay

The total counterpoint to frail social activist groups like APDES in Peru is IPRU in Uruguay. It started out quite small in 1966 and remained so until 1974, but then expanded under new leadership, and has become a multi-pronged organization that is involved in almost every one of the many large-scale cooperative endeavors that are characteristic of certain economic sectors in Uruguay. *Promotores* from IPRU were to be found in almost all the projects I visited in that country, from the dairy cooperative in Durazno to Central Lanera Uruguaya, and from microbusiness enterprises in Montevideo to the alfalfa-growing project in Canelones.

The organization now consists of some thirty professionals and has attracted grant support from Germany, Holland and from U.S. private donors as well as from the Inter-American Foundation. Having a large permanent salaried staff means of course that the organization needs to be alert to "business opportunities." It is probably because he was very much aware of the danger lurking in this situation that a leading member made the emphatic statement: "We are interested in doing *promoción,* not in selling services." Accordingly, IPRU attempts to adhere to three rules: (1) it caters only to low-income groups; (2) it promotes their welfare through efforts at self-help and, above all, mutual help; and (3) it intervenes primarily in the formative stages of various undertakings and withdraws thereafter.

There clearly is something like the "IPRU spirit," a great

La Teja, Montevideo, Uruguay: rebuilding a watch.

GETTING AHEAD COLLECTIVELY

La Teja: rebuilding a motorcycle.

dedication, gentleness, camaraderie. The senior members of the organization have been strongly influenced by the French Dominican Father Lebret who had worked on development problems of Latin America (particularly in Colombia and Brazil) in the fifties and had elaborated a doctrine that attempted to temper economic development with humanist values (the name of both the group and the journal Lebret later founded in France is *Economie et Humanisme*).

Occasionally, the insistence on a collective component of IPRU's development work seemed overdone. Thus IPRU has been active since early 1982 in organizing an association of "microbusinesses" or *microempresas* in a low-income Montevideo barrio by the name of La Teja. We talked there to a micro-industrialist fabricating small transformers and other electrical gadgets, to a watch and alarm clock maker-repairer, and to a mechanic rebuilding old cars. The main need for technical assistance of these small businessmen is in the areas of administration, accounting and finance, especially if they plan on expanding their operations by means of borrowing, and IPRU is

Cali, Colombia: *microempresa* with "boss."

helping in all of these areas. It also has insisted that these microentrepreneurs form an association which holds weekly evening meetings on common concerns. There I wondered (aloud) whether these men and women, with their disparate interests and occupations, would really have enough in common to warrant getting together, week after week. I had not come across similar cooperative requirements in the other well-functioning *microempresas* programs I had visited, in Santo Domingo, Santiago de los Caballeros and Cali. But even though no very clear immediate utility of these weekly meetings emerged from the discussion, my questioning of their value was gently rebuffed: everybody seemed to like those evenings. Perhaps, so I concluded, the electrician, watch maker and mechanic were enjoying them simply as a means of adding a hitherto missing collective or public dimension to their lives.

IPRU's principal activity consists in helping grassroots groups to grow and to become independent and well-established. Generally this task is performed by IPRU's seconding one or several of its staff members on a full or part-time basis to the group that is being assisted. But sometimes IPRU does more than that, as in the case of the "Association of (Land) Settlers of Uruguay" or *Asociación de Colonos del Uruguay* (ACU). In Uruguay, a settler or *colono* is a person who has been given a piece of land (which he has to pay for over a period of years) by the *Instituto Nacional de Colonización*, a government agency that was set up in 1948 and received, particularly in its early years, budgetary appropriations that permitted it to buy large tracts of land from private owners for the purpose of dividing them up among farmers with little or no land. It is a genteel land reform, not wholly inappropriate to the rural scene in Uruguay where pressure on the land by *minifundistas* or landless laborers is much weaker than elsewhere in Latin America. Some five thousand *colono* families have been settled in this manner by the *Instituto* in widely scattered areas over the years, but often their conditions of life and work in the new settlements leave much to be desired. The Institute, not wishing to spend its limited funds on technical assistance and investments in roads and utilities for the *colonos*, sought to stimulate self-help and mutual help among them by founding ACU as part of its own structure, in the early seventies.

ACU prospered and soon became a voice for the *colonos* whose interests were in many ways quite different from those of the Institute (to which, for example, the *colonos* were indebted on account of the land they had received). In view of this conflict of interests, the leaders of the Association decided to leave the protective shell of the Institute and to set up as an independent body. But they needed some outside help to make the transition. Here IPRU came forward not just with technical assistance, but with something far more basic: shelter. Upon separating from the Institute, the Association needed new office space and IPRU offered to house it in its own offices (which happen to be across the street from the Institute) for an interim period. Since then ACU developed vigorously: it established an educational radio program for small farmers, it defended the interests of its members in negotiations about mortgage payments with the Colonization Institute, it has attracted funding from the Inter-American Foundation and from ICCO, the international donor agency of the Dutch Protestant Church, and it has organized annual conventions of *colonos* in Montevideo where official policies are discussed and were strongly criticized last year (shades of ANUC in Colombia, similarly established first by the Government, only to become a vocal and independent peasant union). When I visited ACU, it had just moved again, this time into a small new office of its own. IPRU had done quite well in its nurturing role.

NATIONAL AND INTERNATIONAL AID TO THE GRASSROOTS: AN INTERPRETATION

Apart from its anecdotal interest, the last tale may be symbolic of a deeper meaning: it tells us something about the nature and role of the social activist groups and organizations in contemporary Latin American societies. The Association of Colonists of Uruguay moved from its old offices in a government agency, the Colonization Institute, to new ones in IPRU, one of these activist organizations: is there a suggestion here that IPRU was behaving as a ''state substitute,'' that is, was performing certain functions that were in demand by society, but were not satisfactorily performed by the Uruguayan state? This interpretation of the social activist organizations has much to recommend itself, especially if they are viewed *as a group* and *in conjunction with* the national and international donor organizations, governmental and non-governmental, that channel funds to or through them. It should be mentioned at this point that the Inter-American Foundation is by no means the only international donor that has made contact with the national social activist groups. Many projects and organizations we visited had also received support from such agencies as CARITAS, the international Catholic network for funneling relief, from NOVIB and CEBEMO, the Dutch government and Catholic organizations for overseas aid, respectively, from MISEREOR, the German Catholic group, from OXFAM and other English or Canadian organizations, public and private. In addition, there are the well known American private voluntary organizations such as CARE, Save-the-Children Federation and others which have often become grassroots-development-minded, after having long been concerned primarily with disaster relief.

In other words, there exists today an impressive, loosely integrated network of national and international organizations which, at the level of any single Latin American country, performs important functions of education, public health, housing improvement, agricultural extension, development promotion of handicraft and small business, etc. It is as though both the national and the international conscience about *basic economic rights* of Latin American citizens had outstripped what is provided by the state so that complex substitute or supplementary attempts at assuring these rights have come into being.

The Latin American state itself has contributed to this development by its own oscillatory policies. At some point in the post-war period every one of the six countries dealt with here passed through a reformist phase and undertook new tasks in some areas of social promotion and welfare. A bureacracy was then recruited for this purpose and occasionally the state sponsored semi-independent organizations such as ANUC in Colombia and ACU in Uruguay. Subsequently, this reformist phase is called off or becomes exhausted, retrenchment and reaction set in, and a new government may even wish to undo everything that was done or initiated at the earlier stage. But at this point, a ratchet effect comes into operation. Some of the people recruited into the new bureaucracy will now attempt to do in a private capacity what they were previously paid to do by the government and some of the originally state-sponsored agencies will cut the strings that tied them to officialdom. International funding agencies then are drawn into the vacuum left by the state's default and underwrite a portion of these safeguarding operations. In this manner the actual swing back of social welfare policy, away from what are now considered to be its earlier ''populist excesses'' is, in the end, less violent than it is intended to be. This sort of dynamic, incidentally, is not wholly unknown in the United States. Here also, certain officially sponsored policies of the Johnson Administration's ''War on Poverty'' were continued, when the government withdrew from them, under private auspices, often with the financial support of private foundations.

Nevertheless, the ''normal'' sequence has been rather different in the United States and Europe. Sporadic and local efforts at social promotion and social welfare on the part of agencies founded by wealthy and middle-class individuals with a ''social conscience'' have here often blazed a trail that was eventually followed by comprehensive and systematic governmental initiatives. But this sequence has never functioned satisfactorily in Latin America, perhaps because the chasm between the rich and the poor and the absence of a strong middle class in most of Latin America made abject poverty of the mass of the people appear for a long time as part of the unchangeable order of things. In many instances, it was only the State which could and did achieve initial breakthroughs in the direction of minimal welfare and dignity for the lower classes of society. It is therefore noteworthy that precisely in Latin America private initiatives for social promotion have today come to occupy so prominent a place. The mainspring of these private initiatives is not the "conscience of the educated and the rich" as was the case in Western Europe and North America before the advent of the contemporary Welfare State, but *a combination of social activism at the local and national levels, inspired by a great variety of ideologies, with the conscience of some of the rich countries at the international level.* This configuration makes of course for many awkard problems, misunderstandings, and inefficiencies. But it has permitted the grassroots movement in Latin America to proceed with a minimum of paternalism, perhaps because of the distance between the donors and the ultimate beneficiaries, and with much inventiveness, no doubt because of its decentralized and pluralist nature.

Chapter Seven

What Does It All Add Up To?

The last few pages make it easier to speculate on the grand question that is bound to be asked by at least one set of readers (not, I might add, the more likable one): "what does it all add up to, what difference does it make?" The first reaction to this question by those who have actually been to the sites and listened to the people involved in the various efforts and movements here described is an indignant refusal to entertain it at all: why not be satisifed with "saving souls," that is, with rejoicing over whatever advances in human welfare, solidarity and hope are being achieved, without attempting the impossible task of summing up all these efforts, successful or disappointing, and of comparing the resulting "total" to some equally nebulous concept such as the General Economic Welfare or the Prospects for Democracy?

There is much to recommend such a refusal. The whole venture of grassroots development has arisen in good measure from a revulsion against the worship of the "gross national product" and of the "rate of growth" as unique arbiters of economic and human progress. Grassroots development refuses to be judged by these standards. The workers in this vineyard look at their activity as valuable in itself without regard to its "overall" impact and they do quite well without being reassured at every step by optimistic reports on the macroeconomic consequences of their work.

With respect to political effects, participants in grassroots development are similarly convinced that there is something illusory about the importance widely attributed to the large-scale political changes—the swinging of the pendulum from autocratic authoritarianism to more or less democratic forms and back again—that have been characteristic of so many countries for so long in Latin America. They are convinced that for political conditions to change more fundamentally, a great many social, cultural and even personal relationships must become transformed. In this respect, they are at one with François Furet, the historian of the French Revolution and of its historiography, who has recently written about the strange "consensus [stemming from the Revolution] according to which any aspiration to social change implies, for *all* groups [on the Left and the Right] the prior seizure of the central power of the state." And he adds, in a final arresting sentence: "Perhaps it is this heritage that is being questioned today."[17]

Perhaps it is also being questioned in Latin America, precisely by the grassroots movement. The decision of many middle class professionals to work for the social activist groups is a case in point. When I first came to know Latin America thirty-two years ago, the only possibility for a young man with a university degree to make his way (in contrast to today, there were then very few women with such degrees) was to embark on a routine business, professional, or perhaps, political career. To choose such a career implied a decision to bolster the existing order. Some ten years later, additional possibilities had appeared: you could become a *técnico* working for some reform from within a central government office, or a guerrilla fighting the "system" from without. Then, after another decade, in the seventies and eighties, yet a further possible course opened up for some of Latin America's restless middle-class youth: becoming a *promotor social* whose task it is to build self-help communities at the grassroots and thus to achieve human betterment and social change in a less spectacular, but perhaps more fundamental manner.

In spite of my initial protestations, I have now come up with a partial answer to the question asked in the title of this chapter, for the availability of this new option for a highly influential

---

[17] "La Révolution dans l'imaginaire politique français," *Le Débat*, No. 26, (September 1983), p. 181. Guillermo O'Donnell has similarly and eloquently argued that to consolidate the renascent democracy in Argentina it is necessary to democratize social interaction at various micro levels. See his "Democracia en la Argentina: *micro* y *macro*," (October 1983, mimeo).

GETTING AHEAD COLLECTIVELY

group of people is in itself an important sociological and political fact that "makes a difference." Not that the newly opening "careers" will necessarily draw people away from the guerrilla path: they could just as well gather their recruits primarily from among those who would otherwise have pursued traditional professional or business careers or become attracted by the possibility of joining the reformist *técnicos*. But this much is certain: the lives of Latin American middle-class youth have been enriched by the opening up of this vast new area of possible endeavors.

What about the impact of the grassroots projects, associations and movements themselves? A dense network of such movements, jointly with a large number of social activist organizations, is bound to change the traditional character of Latin American society in several ways, most of which are not yet well understood.[18] But it seems safe to assert that, with such a network, social relations become *more caring* and *less private*. Now we know that certain types of regimes depend for their stability and untrammeled authority on the thorough *privatization* of their citizens' lives. Many years ago, a political scientist noted a crucial difference between totalitarian regimes such as those of Hitler, Mussolini and Stalin, and authoritarian regimes such as that of Franco's Spain in the decades after World War II: in totalitarian regimes the masses of the people are kept in a constant state of mobilization—in Mussolini's Italy, this was epitomized by the saying "We Italians are condemned to live in a state of permanent enthusiasm"—whereas in authoritarian regimes the masses are demobilized to the greatest possible extent.[19] Demobilization means privatization: everyone is to be concerned exclusively with his own welfare and that of his immediate family. Now some contemporary or recent non-democratic regimes in Latin America are

[18] A thoughtful contribution is in Ruth C. L. Cardoso, "Movimentos sociais urbanos: balanço critico" in Bernardo Sorj and Maria Herminia Tavares Almeida, eds., *Sociedade e Politica no Brasil* (São Paulo: Brasiliense, 1983), pp. 215–239.

[19] Juan Linz, "An Authoritarian Regime: The Case of Spain" in Erik Allard and Stein Rokkan, eds., *Mass Politics: Studies in Political Sociology* (New York: The Free Press, 1970). This article was first published in 1964. Its distinction between authoritarian and totalitarian regimes is very different from the one later drawn by Jeane Kirkpatrick. The entire distinction has been questioned in the recent notable article by Michael Walzer, "On Failed Totalitarianism," *Dissent* (Summer 1983), pp. 297–306.

CONCLUSION

or have been of the mobilization (or would-be mobilization) type: illustrations are Perón's Argentina, Velasco's Peru, Fidel Castro's Cuba and now the Sandinista regime in Nicaragua. But the major authoritarian wave of the sixties and seventies in Brazil, Chile, Uruguay and Argentina definitely attempted to defuse mass mobilization and to turn the citizens into very private persons. In principle, the formation of cooperatives and other forms of collective action at the grassroots should therefore be incompatible with the very structural requirements of those authoritarian regimes. Perhaps these movements can then claim some credit for the recent weakening and retreats of these regimes which, with all the might and frightfulness at their command, and with their pretensions to introduce a stable new order, seem to have a lifespan of at most ten years?

It is of course impossible to prove such a connection. Moreover, in two major countries, Argentina and Chile, powerful proximate causes—the defeat in the Falklands and a particularly severe economic downturn, respectively—account satisfactorily for the political crises and changes of 1982—83. Nevertheless, it is conceivable that the grassroots stirrings, together with the searchings of the social activists, were an important underlying factor in preventing the social quiescence and introversion that are required for an authoritarian regime to take hold.

In any event, some surprise is occasioned by the willingness of such regimes to tolerate both the grassroots movements and the social activist organizations that are attempting to ''stir up'' such movements and stand ready to assist them. It must be noted right away that the tolerance was by no means limitless. Under the Trujillo dictatorship in the Dominican Republic, rural cooperatives were harassed and largely suppressed. In Pinochet's Chile, cooperatives of small peasants were forced for a while to affiliate with the cooperatives of medium and large farmers; the intention was to drown out their independent voice and personality. In Argentina, the slum clearance projects of the military government in the late seventies were organized as surprise operations so that any kind of collective response and resistance was virtually ruled out. Nevertheless, the weight of repression of the authoritarian regimes was directed against labor unions as well as against those cooperative arrangements in agriculture that had arisen directly from land expropriations undertaken by previous governments. Other,

GETTING AHEAD COLLECTIVELY

often minor cooperative initiatives involving consumer stores, agricultural inputs and produce, or vocational training and educational ventures in city slums slipped by the vigilance of the authorities. It is of course conceivable that, just as such ventures are often considered as "diversionary" by the Left, so they were welcomed by the new authoritarian regimes as social formations likely to absorb energies that might otherwise take more dangerous forms. Basically, however, most of these ventures probably were not bothered because they were directed so blatantly at that unexceptionable and seemingly harmless Smithian objective: to "better people's condition." Little did the authorities realize that, as shown in our stories, that very effort could turn into what from their point of view is a dangerous Trojan Horse.

Thus it came about that in some countries the grassroots movements and the related social activist organizations experienced sustained growth while repressive and authoritarian governments were holding power. The best and no doubt most important known case is that of Brazil[20] with its Catholic grassroots movement known as *Comunidades Ecclesiasticas de Base* (CEB). These *Comunidades* multiplied in the seventies and played a significant role in the eventual "opening" (*abertura*) of the Brazilian political system and in the partial return of that country to pluralist forms.[21] But on the much smaller scale of Uruguay, an analogous story has been unfolding. Here, IPRU's expansion dates from 1974, one year after the formal installation of an outstandingly repressive military regime and almost all the cooperative grassroots programs with which IPRU has been associated grew steadily during that period. All of these groups share an almost visceral dislike of authoritarian rule and their rise is a factor in the (painfully slow) return of Uruguay to more democratic governance.

In countries currently enjoying pluralist politics—Colombia, Peru, and the Dominican Republic in our sample—a dense network of grassroots movements and social activist organizations tends to reinforce those politics. In addition to mutual help and collective effort, grassroots movements always have a com-

[20] I have not dealt with Brazil in this essay because the Inter-American Foundation has not been active in Brazil during recent years.

[21] See Paul Singer and Vinicius Caldeira Brant, eds., *O Povo em Movimento* (Petrópolis: Vozes, 1981). Chapter 3.

ponent that consists of requests for assistance (with regard to title to land, public utilities, credit facilities, etc.) addressed to local authorities or official agencies. In a democratic state, this sort of mobilization can lead to active exchanges and bargaining among the voters, the parties, the candidates for office and the elected representatives, and therefore to a more vital interaction between top and base. True, the resulting politics can become narrowly focused on local issues and politicians will often be able to buy a whole group of votes by promising—and delivering—some special favor to a grassroots organization. In Cristo Rey in Colombia, for example (See Chapter 4), a particularly fine fishing net had been nicknamed the "Belisario net" because its purchase became possible—so we were told—through a "donation" made to the cooperative during the 1982 Presidential election campaign by representatives of Belisario Betancur, the present President of Colombia.

But this sort of incident is only one of several manifestations of the increased influence poor people can wield by becoming organized in a society where politicians must be responsive to the voters. Another possible direction is illustrated, also in Colombia, by the decision of a group of beneficiaries of the Inter-American Foundation to call a conference during which the various experiences of distinct grassroots groups of the country would be canvassed. One such conference, with 24 groups represented, was held in 1982 and a second one, with over fifty groups, took place the following year. The stated objective of such conferences is to promote mutual learning from each other's experiences as well as common projects and exchanges. But such gatherings could do more and create a new voice for many hitherto submerged groups of society, a voice that would give these groups a stake in the pluralist state.

As noted in the last chapter, the growth of collective action for economic advance at the grassroots and of the associated complex of local, national and international organizations extending professional and financial assistance may simply be a reflection of an increasing and increasingly difficult-to-deny recognition of basic economic rights to be extended to all citizens. Perhaps we are in the presence of a worldwide trend, for a similar movement appears to be sweeping India. In an article about the rising star of a new politician, Chandra Shekhar, a reporter writes in *The New York Times:* "Mr. Shekhar said that he planned to begin a cooperative effort with social activist groups who are administering programs ranging from environmental protection to health care, all aimed at bettering the lives of the poor. Political science forecasters say that there are thousands of such groups which make up a decentralized movement in what is a decentralized society. They say that social activism is moving into the vacuum left by the decay of other political institutions.''[22]

At this point it might be asked why grassroots movements should become more numerous, active and vocal at a time when there is a great deal of talk about a new set of human rights to basic subsistence, education, health care, a safe environment, and participation in decision-making, in addition to such older human rights as freedom of religion, expression, movement and so on. Why would the increasingly widespread consciousness about these new rights not have the effect of making people relax, as long as all they seemingly have to do is to wait for these rights to fall into their lap? To think so would be to profoundly misjudge the conditions under which people are likely to engage upon a new and perhaps risky course—such as collective action—to ''better their condition.'' They will do so precisely once they feel that better condition to be not just desirable, but to be *a thing rightfully theirs* of which they are deprived. This is the reason why the proclamation of a right has so often been, if not automatically self-fulfilling, at least the first step to any serious attempt to secure that right.

The wide distance separating the actual conditions of life of countless Latin Americans from what is increasingly felt as the conditions to which they have a *right* is the source of the enormous tensions in that continent; at the same time, it is the mainspring of the manifold local efforts at overcoming that distance—efforts I have found inspiring to visit and absorbing to record.

[22] *The New York Times* (June 27, 1983).